Designs for Active Learning

A Sourcebook of Classroom Strategies for Information Education

Edited by
Gail Gradowski
Santa Clara University, Santa Clara, California

Loanne Snavely
Pennsylvania State University, University Park, Pennsylvania

Paula Dempsey
DePaul University Library, Chicago, Illinois

Production editor:
Kevin M. Roddy

With the
Teaching Methods Committee
Instruction Section
Association of College & Research Libraries

Association of College & Research Libraries
A Division of the American Library Association
Chicago 1998

Library of Congress Cataloging-in-Publication Data

Designs for active learning : a sourcebook of classroom strategies for
   information education / edited by Gail Gradowski, Loanne Snavely,
   Paula Dempsey ; production editor, Kevin M. Roddy ; with the
   Teaching Methods Committee, Instruction Section, Association of
   College & Research Libraries.
       p.   cm.
   Includes bibliographical references.
   ISBN 0-8389-7946-7 (alk. paper)
   1. Library orientation for college students--United States.
2. Active learning--United States. I. Gradowski, Gail.
II. Snavely, Loanne. III. Dempsey, Paula. IV. Association of
College and Research Libraries. Instruction Section. Teaching
Methods Committee.
Z711.2.D47   1998
025.5'677--dc21   98-7100

Printed in the United States of America.

02 01 00 99 98   5 4 3 2 1

Contents

Section II: Searching Indexes and Online Catalogs 59

Edited by William Orme and Kevin M. Roddy

Section III: Search Strategies for the Research Process   145
Edited by Gail Gradowski and Loanne Snavely

Section IV: Evaluation of Library Resources   159
Edited by Michael Blake and Ed Tallent

Section V: Discipline-Oriented Instruction 193
Edited by Gail Gradowski

Active Learning in the Library Instruction Classroom

Years ago, a master teacher and the winner of a national award for teaching excellence referred to teaching as a "sweaty-palmed business." While I knew the feeling only too well myself, I was surprised to find that even well known and successful "good" teachers say that teaching is hard work, that enormous amounts of preparation are required to make it appear effortless and spontaneous, and that one can never know for sure if a class will be a resounding success or a dismal failure. How can such uncertainty be part of good teaching? Because student's active participation and learning are variables in the equation of good teaching.

This active engagement helps students integrate new material with what they already know. It helps them formulate new ideas in their own words and it helps students with a variety of learning styles understand the material in ways they would not if it was delivered in a lecture format. In short, it increases student's learning. If this is our ultimate goal, which it should be, then we should seek ways to actively engage students in the classroom. But this is not easy, and in fact, it requires learning on the part of the teacher. The teacher no longer has total control, and can no longer rely on a prepared lecture for success. Student responses and dynamics will vary from class to class, and may produce the unexpected. We, as teachers, must be ready to respond, and to guide the learning toward the desired goal.

Although teachers in the active learning classroom do not have total control, much can be done to ensure the success of the class. Proponents of collaborative and cooperative learning have shown us that success is most often achieved by carefully structuring the sessions. Asking for a general discussion rarely works, usually producing either no response, or quickly rambling off-topic and wasting class time. But asking students to think for a moment about a particular question relevant to the topic, then share their ideas with one partner for a minute or two, and then collect responses from the class, will invariably produce an excellent list of relevant ideas. This is an exercise known as "think-pair-share" and is one of many techniques designed to provide structure to efficiently and actively engage students in their own learning.

In the past, library instruction has often been teacher-centered and lecture-oriented. As librarians have pursued the goal of making their teaching more active and student-centered, they have not only read the literature, but have participated in workshops and conferences with other teaching faculty. Bringing this excitement into the library instruction classroom has presented many challenges. Frequently asked questions include: How do these techniques translate for my teaching? What can I actually do in my classroom? How do I get started?

These are the questions this sourcebook on active learning techniques is designed to answer. It has been prepared for those who have an understanding of active learning theory and techniques, but who are looking for assistance in implementing these in their teaching. This sourcebook is a collection of classroom strategies that have been developed and used success-fully by creative librarians in their own teaching. They are shared here so that others can use them. They can be followed just as they are, or used as models to adapt to the needs, topics and unique situations of individual classes at particular institutions.

Trying active learning for the first time may be intimidating. The success of the class depends not only on the advance preparation, which is in the teachers control, but on the students' responses and dynamics, which are not. Success also depends on the ability of the teacher to guide the class through the active learning exercise to achieve the desired result. A librarian introducing active learning techniques for the first time, may want to "start small" and begin with a short exercise that can be introduced into a predominately lecture class. Several strat-egies that take only five or ten minutes are included here. As success is gained with these brief exercises, it will be easier to try longer and more involved exercises. A wide variety of "reci-pes" have been selected to cover a range of teaching needs, and include both short and long time frames, simple and complex exercises, and a variety of techniques and topics.

For those who have not been exposed to active learning previously, a selected reading list is provided. It includes works on active learning from those who were at the forefront of its development in college teaching, as well as those who have introduced it to librarianship. Bonwell and Eison's *Active Learning: Creating Excitement in the Classroom* (1991) is an excellent introduction to what it is, research on its use, and how to get started. This is probably the best place to start an exploration of the topic. Many others are available, including *Striving for Excellence in College: Tips for Active Learning* (Browne, 1997) and *Using Active Learning in College Classes* (Sutherland and Bonwell, 1996).

In addition to works specifically on active learning, a number of related areas are essential for introducing active learning into the classroom. Gronlund (1995) discusses the importance of establishing clear objectives, including objectives related to intellectual, affective, and perfor-mance outcomes as well as overall instructional objectives. Once these are established, Weston and Cranton (1986), and Meyers and Jones (1993) are helpful sources for identifying and selecting classroom strategies that will help meet those objectives. Grasha (1996) provides an overview of learning styles, teaching styles, and classroom processes, and discusses their inter-dependence. Detailed descriptions of over 40 methods of instruction and their use to en-courage active learning are presented. Cross and Steadman (1996) and Menges and Weiner (1997) stress the importance of examining the research on teaching and learning to find out what is really enhancing learning, and implementing that research in the classroom. Assess-ment is critical to ensuring that classroom methods are working. Cross and Angelo (1993) cover all aspects of assessing teaching effectiveness and the learning that occurs in the class-room.

A number of authors have brought the active learning issue into the library literature. Ridgeway (1989a) discusses the difficulty in changing teaching styles from one that is primarily lecture to one that involves active learning. She emphasizes that a major change of teaching style cannot happen through one workshop, but requires preparation, training, and practice over a longer period of time. She provides suggestions and further resources to aid librarians in this difficult transition and stresses the importance of collegiality and peer coaching in the process. In another article, "Integrating Active Learning Techniques into the One-Hour Bibliographic Instruction Lecture," Ridgeway (1989b) emphasizes the librarian's role in facilitating student's learning. Allen (1995) provides a brief overview of active learning, from it's roots in the Socratic method to the present. Bodi (1990) relates learning styles to library instruction. Fister (1990) introduces collaborative learning, while Hanson (1995), a writing instructor, discusses its use and relevance for librarians. Some successful uses of active learning techniques in the library classroom include the use of cooperative learning (Cook, et al., 1995); student journals to tell a story (Jacobson and Mark, 1995); a small scale introduction of active learning to a lecture class (Drueke, 1992); and a large scale introduction of active learning to over 5,000 students using Graduate Teaching Assistants (Williams and Cox, 1992). Whitmore (1996, 1997) provides examples of hands-on activities for library instruction and use of the internet.

These resources will help in gaining an understanding of the theory and practice of active learning. This sourcebook is intended to help librarians with the next step: the implementation of these strategies in the classroom.

Loanne Snavely, October 2, 1997

Selected Readings

Allen, E. (1995). Active learning and teaching: Improving postsecondary library instruction. *The Reference Librarian, 51–52*, 89–103.

Angelo, T. A., ed. (1991). *Classroom research: Early lessons from success.* San Francisco: Jossey-Bass.

Bodi, S. (1990). Teaching effectiveness and bibliographic instruction: The relevance of learning styles. *College and Research Libraries* 51, 113–119.

Bonwell, C. C., & Eison, J. A. (1991). *Active learning, creating excitement in the classroom.* Washington, D.C.: School of Education and Human Development, George Washington University.

Browne, M. N. (1997). *Striving for excellence in college: Tips for active learning.* Upper Saddle River, N.J.: Prentice Hall.

Cook, K. N., Kunkel, L. R., & Weaver, S. M. (1995). Cooperative learning in bibliographic instruction. *Research Strategies, 13*, 17–25.

Cross, K. P., & Angelo, T. A. (1988). *Classroom assessment techniques: A handbook for faculty.* Ann Arbor: National Center for Research to Improve Postsecondary Teaching and Learning.

Cross, K. P., & Steadman, M. H. (1996). *Classroom research: Implementing the scholarship of teaching.* San Francisco: Jossey-Bass.

Drueke, J. (1992). Active learning in the university library instruction classroom. *Research Strategies, 10*, 77–83.

Fister, B. (1990). Teaching research as a social act: Collaborative learning and the library. *RQ* 29, 505–09.

Grasha, A. F. (1996). *Teaching with style: A practical guide to enhancing learning by understanding teaching and learning styles.* Pittsburgh: Alliance.

Gronlund, N. E. (1995). *How to write and use instructional objectives.* 5th ed. Englewood Cliffs, NJ: Prentice Hall.

Hanson, M. (1995). Joining the conversation: Collaborative learning and bibliographic instruction. *The Reference Librarian, 51–52*, 147–59.

Jacobson, T. E., & Mark, B. L. (1995). Teaching in the information age: Active learning techniques to empower students. *The Reference Librarian, 51–52,* 105–20.

Menges, R. J., & Weimer, M. (1996). *Teaching on solid ground: Using scholarship to improve practice.* San Francisco: Jossey-Bass.

Meyers, C., & Jones, T. B. (1993). *Promoting active learning: Strategies for the college classroom.* San Francisco: Jossey-Bass.

Ridgeway, T. (1989a). Changing teaching styles. *RQ 29,* 24–27.

Ridgeway, T. (1989b). Integrating active learning technologies into the online bibliographic instruction lecture. In G. E. Mensching & T. B. Mensching (Eds.) *Coping with information illiteracy: Bibliographic instruction for the information age.* Ann Arbor: Pierian Press.

Sutherland, T. E., & Bonwell, C. C. (1996). *Using active learning in college classes: A range of options for faculty.* San Francisco: Jossey-Bass.

Weston, C., & Cranton, P. A. (1986). Selecting Instructional Strategies. *Journal of Higher Education 57,* 259–88.

Whitmore, M. P., ed. (1996). *Empowering students; Hands-on library instruction activities.* Pittsburgh: Library Instruction Publications.

Whitmore, M. P., ed. (1997). *Unmasking the internet for research: Using hands-on active learning exercises.* Pittsburgh: Library Instruction Publications.

Williams, K., & Cox, J. (1992). Active learning in action. *RQ 31,* 326–31.

A History of the Project with Acknowledgments

A project by committee and task force to compile exercises such as this sourcebook is an enormous undertaking involving many people. Its development, from the initial idea to the final product, is worth mentioning, and I will briefly review it here.

In 1991, one of the first projects of the newly formed BIS standing committee, the Teaching Methods Committee, was affectionately known as "position papers." Under the leadership of committee chair Randy Hensley, members of the committee chose topics of interest to them that involved a new method or aspect of teaching and wrote a two to three page synopsis of the topic and appended a selected bibliography. The purpose of these papers was to educate ourselves about what was happening in higher education regarding teaching methods, and to briefly demonstrate its place in library instruction. Several of these papers, including Margie Wells' on "Active Learning", mine on "Collaborative Learning," Andrea Bartelstein's on "Adult Learning Theory" and Jody Caldwell's on "Learning Cycles," generated a new discussion. The discussion centered around incorporating active learning techniques into the library classroom. In our experience, the primary teaching method used by librarians was lecture and/or demonstration. Even those who had some training in active learning techniques felt that it was difficult to translate these methods into the library instruction classroom. Models and examples of exercises that worked in the classroom were needed to help bridge the gap. The discussion led to the next project. Jody Caldwell and Alphonse Vinh coordinated the call for "active learning scenarios", requesting librarians who used such techniques in their classrooms to send a brief description of their in-class exercises and any handouts that they used. The submissions that were received were copied and compiled into a packet. Meanwhile, as another committee project, Cindy Faries was compiling an up-to-date list of state and regional organizations devoted to library instruction. In order to get them into the hands of those who might use them, the packets were distributed to the contact persons for each organization with a request that they be shared at the local, state and regional level. A packet was also sent to LOEX. The committee successfully completed the "Active Learning Scenario" Project, and moved on to other activities.

As the next chair of the Teaching Methods committee, I discovered that the project had generated its own success. Librarians heard about it and wanted to see it, or wanted a copy. The LOEX copy was not sufficient, and the committee continued to receive requests. Several problems arose. The packet was large and costly to duplicate and mail. All submissions had been copied exactly as they were received, and with e-mail technology what it was in the early 90's this meant that some were copies of hastily written messages, printed out screen by screen; others were printed on poor quality dot matrix printers that didn't reproduce well. Electronic versions of the messages had not been saved. While this had been part of the design of the original project, to collect the scenarios quickly and get them to the grass roots users, it made ongoing distribution of the packet difficult. The committee enthusiastically decided to create a "second edition." Enough time had passed that more active learning was being tried in the classroom, and there was a sense that there were more exercises out there to collect. The committee began exploring possible avenues of publication. We envisioned a compilation similar to a SPEC kit, and explored a number of possibilities, eventually calling it among ourselves "the cookbook". Our ideas didn't really fit into any of these other formats, so we decided to submit it as a monograph to ACRL. A detailed, five page proposal for "Active Learning: A Sourcebook of Classroom Strategies for Information Education" outlined our objectives, the scope and content of the project, its history and so forth. The proposal was submitted first to BIS Executive committee. Upon approval, it was forwarded to the ACRL publications committee, where it received an enthusiastic response and the permission to proceed with the project as an ACRL Publication.

At this point, Gail Gradowski assumed leadership of the committee's activities. A call for "recipes" went out and the resulting submissions were prepared and copied for blind review. The entire committee acted as peer reviewers in a blind referee process at ALA midwinter meeting in 1996 to select the best of the entries. Our criteria included the need for each accepted entry to engage students actively in the classroom. Or if students were sent off with an exercise to complete, a follow-up component with the teacher to analyze and review results was required. When multiple entries were very similar, the best examples were selected. But when similar entries included variations that would be useful in differing situations, more than one was included. The committee divided the accepted entries up into logical chapter divisions and assigned chapters to volunteers from the committee. Upon examining our accepted entries, the committee felt there were still gaps that needed to be filled. Certain topics and techniques were well represented, while others were totally absent or sparsely represented. We decided to do a second call, specifying certain areas in which we desired entries. The responses from the second call were also reviewed, and all accepted entries were divided up into the existing chapter divisions. After the annual conference in 1996, the Active Learning Sourcebook Task Force was established to carry on the project. The chapter editors communicated with those who submitted the exercises, brought each exercise into a standardized format so that basic information would be presented for each exercise, and wrote chapter introductions. A few exercises received their original editing by someone other than the chapter editors. These include Elizabeth Hanson for exercises 11, 12, 13, and 29; Fannette Thomas for exercise 21; Janet Reit for exercise 49; Paula Dempsey for exercises 50 and 52; Michael Blake for exercise 48; and Ed Tallent for exercise 54.

The editors wish to thank all of the committee members who helped with the project, and the author/teachers whose classroom strategies are compiled here and without whom the entire project would not have been possible.

Loanne Snavely

Teaching Methods Committee Members, 1994–1996

Marilee Birchfield	1994–95	Ann Pederson	1994–95
Michael Blake	1994–96	Linda B. Paez	1995–96
Jody L. Caldwell	1994–95	Loanne Snavely	
Paula R. Dempsey	1995–96	Chair	1993–95
Gail A. Gradowski		Stephanie F. Race	1995–96
Member	1994–95	Janet W. Reit	1994–96
Chair	1995–96	Trish Ridgeway	1995–96
Elizabeth I. Hanson	1995–96	Kevin M. Roddy	1995–96
Xiaoyang Liu	1995–96	Edward P. Tallent	1995–96
William A. Orme	1994–96	Fanette H. Thomas	1995–96

Active Learning Sourcebook Task Force Members, 1996–98

Paula Dempsey	1996–98
Gail Gradowski	
Chair	1996–98
Trish Ridgeway	1996–98
Loanne Snavely	1996–98

Kevin M. Roddy	
Production Editor	1996–97

Section I

Basic Library Instruction

Edited by Paula R. Dempsey and Janet W. Reit

Library orientations and other introductory sessions often sag under the weight of too much lecturing and not enough active learning. This section provides examples of active learning exercises that enhance basic introduction to the library and its resources. The techniques presented include stimulating small group discussions, cooperative assignments with wrap-up oral reports, lectures designed by students, as well as more structured exercises that engage students and motivate them to learn.

The objectives of a session on basic library instruction are necessarily broad and may include a variety of objectives. Students will be exposed to the range of resources available in an academic library, which are often much different from libraries they have used in the past. Sessions should motivate students by giving them a taste of the wealth of material available on any topic, both within and outside a specific institution. Students need to become familiar with the physical layout and the intellectual organization of the library. Students must understand the necessity for developing a specific, manageable research topic. It is also important for students to be comfortable asking a librarian for assistance.

The problems of basic sessions lie in their general nature. Often, students in basic library instruction session have not been assigned a research project and do not have a research topic in mind. The recipes in this chapter provide ideas for focusing the session on interesting topics. The activities also provide ways to motivate students to participate in applying the new knowledge so they will be able to draw on it for future research projects.

Librarians who are new to active learning techniques might benefit from a structured approach such as the "Library-ese Glossary Exercise." More experienced instructors might want to experiment with a more open-ended technique like "Structuring a Session with Questions." Most of the activities will work best with relatively small classes, but the "Active Response to Information through an Internal Class Newsgroup" would work equally well with a large, geographically dispersed group.

1. Active Response to Information through an Internal Class Newsgroup

Janet McNeil Hurlbert
Snowden Library, Lycoming College, Williamsport, Pennsylvania

Introduction	This activity uses an on-campus newsgroup to extend the library instruction session throughout the course in an active way.
Subject	Any specialized subject area, especially in upper-division courses
Level of Activity	Advanced
Time Required	30–60 minutes per week for the number of weeks students are working on the research assignment
Size of Class	Any
Preparation	1. Have the campus computer center set up an internal newsgroup for students in the class. (All students must have e-mail accounts.) 2. Work with the course instructor to develop information activities related to the research project and deadlines for completing them. 3. At agreed upon times in the course, post the information activity instructions to the class newsgroup and monitor the results.
Class Instructions	At certain times throughout this course, information assignments will be posted to the class newsgroup to which you must respond. The activities will be related to the research project for the course and will serve as a way for you to explore the information resources available in the library and on the Internet. They will give you the opportunity to share discoveries with your classmates and learn from what other students have discovered.

Examples of the information assignments would be as follows:
• Find an article that further explains topic X, which we discussed in class today. Post three new points that you learned about the topic through your reading. Do you agree with the conclusion of the article?
• Find an article about *person X*. What four questions would you like to ask him or her, based on the information presented in the article?

- Answer two of the questions posted by your classmates about *person X*, based on your research about this person's life.

You may also post questions to the class newsgroup for the librarian to answer about the research projects you are working on, as well as tips about research for your classmates about saving time in the library or on the Internet.

Discussion

This activity requires a close working relationship with the classroom instructor to establish what kinds of informational questions will be required of the students and how many will be required. In addition, students should be required to use the newsgroup through a grade or other means of evaluation. It also is important for the librarian to be willing to follow the newsgroup and intervene with information for the list, or to send information to the individual student who posted a request for information.

2. Classification Brainstorming

Colleen Bell
University of Oregon, Eugene, Oregon

Introduction

A concrete example of the complexity of classification can give students a conceptual framework for understanding Library of Congress or Dewey Decimal Classification. The activity is based on a chapter from Richard Saul Wurman's *Information Anxiety*, in which he discusses five basic ways of organizing information: category, time, location, alphabet, and continuum. Discussing the implications of organizational decisions provides students with skills they can use in any library, regardless of its classification system.

Subject

Any

Level of Activity

Basic

Time Required

50 minutes

Size of Class

Up to 20 (3–5 groups of 3–4 students each)

Preparation

1. One week before the session, put on reserve or distribute copies of Richard Saul Wurman, *Information Anxiety* (New York: Doubleday, 1989), Chapter 2, "The Understanding Business," pp. 51–82.
2. Gather a set of small, varied objects for classification (e.g., stuffed toys, postcards, canned foods, children's picture books, kitchen tools).

Class Instructions

In this session, we will apply the ideas from the assigned reading to a concrete example. You will have 10 minutes to take this set of items and classify them in as many ways as you can. Try to apply all five of the basic ways of organizing information: category, time, location, alphabet, and continuum. You will also discuss with your group the benefits of the specific means of organization and under what circumstances you would want to use a particular classification.

Discussion

1. Organize students into several small groups.
2. Start the class with a 5-minute discussion of the five ways of organizing information. Ask students to propose examples of each method that are used in their daily lives.

3. Give each group a number of related items, and allow the students 10 minutes to "classify" the objects based on the five ways, moving the objects around and arranging them as needed. Circulate to answer questions and observe discussions.

4. Have each group present the various classifications they came up with and the advantages and disadvantages of each one for various purposes.

5. Lead the students into a 5-minute discussion of the ways library materials can be organized.

6. Introduce the LCC and DDC systems, emphasizing the system used at your institution.

7. Explain the purpose and use of call numbers in classifying library materials.

3.   Crime and Punishment

Gail Gradowski,
Orradre Library, Santa Clara University, Santa Clara, California

Introduction

These timed exercises are designed to keep students engaged and moving. Students work in groups and have 10-15 minutes to complete each exercise. Each group receives one set of color-coded envelopes that contain exercise sheets. Students work on the exercises until they hear a timer ring or are asked to stop. Each group passes its envelope and unused exercise sheets to the next table, and everyone begins again on a new set of exercises.

Students will need to have easy access to the online catalog (OSCAR on the work sheets) and other databases used during the class.

Subject

First-year writing course

Level of Activity

Undergraduate

Time Required

Class time: 65–105 minutes; Preparation time: several hours to adapt and copy handouts and prepare envelopes.

Size of Class

20–25 students

Preparation

1. Arrange furniture so that there are eight tables in 2 sets of 4, with enough surrounding space so that 3 people could sit at each table.
2. Flag the tables with numbers 1 through 8.
3. Gather the worksheets and other materials for the 4 tasks:
   - 8 copies of the worksheet, Watch Your Language (Figure 3-1), in 2 piles of 4.
   - 8 copies of the worksheet, Where Exactly Will I Find These? (Figure 3-2), in 2 piles of 4.
   - 8 copies of the worksheet, More I Want More (Figure 3-3), in 2 piles of 4.
   - 2 book covers to go along with More I Want More.
   - 4 copies of each of the 2 different versions of Who's Speaking Please (Figure 3-4).
   - The 4 periodicals that go along with each of the 2 versions of Who's Speaking Please.

- 6 copies of the handout, Types of Periodicals, (Figure 3-5) 3 to go with each version of Who's Speaking Please.
- 8 large envelopes.(It helps to color code these in 2 sets of 4 so that you can refer to the groupings of 4 as "the yellow group" and the other as "the blue group.")

4. Prepare the 8 envelopes. In each set of 4, you should have 1 envelope containing 4 copies of Watch Your Language, 1 envelope containing 4 copies of Where Exactly Will I Find These, 1 envelope containing 4 copies of More, I Want More and 1 envelope containing 4 copies of Who's Speaking Please (2 different versions).

5. Put one envelope and any accompanying other material (see the list above) at each table, making sure that the color-coordinated sets are at adjacent tables.

Class Instructions

As students enter give them a "seat assignment" number designating one of the eight tables.

After introducing yourself, in very speedy fashion, give them a very general "lay of the land" description of what is about to transpire, e.g. "You will be working in groups on 4 timed exercises that will expand your skills at using the online catalog and a computerized periodical index and at discriminating between different types of periodicals as information sources." Explain briefly how it will all work, e.g., "You are either a yellow group or a blue group. You will work on one copy of the exercise in the envelope at your table for 12 minutes. At the end of that time, a timer will go off and you will pass the envelope with the remaining blank exercise sheets as well as any other material, like the periodicals, to the next table in your color group."

Instruct them to take out the first exercise sheet and begin. Remind them to read the instructions carefully.

Start the timer!

As they work, go around and assist. Their instructor will, hopefully, do the same.

Discussion

After all 4 tasks have been done by all the groups, briskly review the answers as a class. Have ready for each exercise a list of points you wish to make and questions you want to ask so that you will not get bogged down on one or two questions. The exercises are designed so that the most important points should be made in the groups while the students are working.

For the 65-minute classes, you can afford to allow only 10 minutes per task if you want to have time left over to review the answers. Even then, it is cutting it short, so have your "review the answers" part well planned to get to the most important points.

For the 105-minute classes, you can afford 15 minutes per task, unless you have something especially lengthy to do afterward. These classes may continue with time for students to work on their own topics using various other worksheets available for that purpose.

FIGURE 3-1

Watch your language!

99.9% of the time there is more than one way
to look up a topic on a computer.
Furthermore, unless you are a highly skilled librarian, odds are about
99 to 1 that you won't hit on the best way right away!

Consider this topic:

LEGALIZATION OF MARIJUANA

A savvy searcher would do a **KEYWORD** search on OSCAR, starting with the most obvious words:

legalization marijuana

A critical searcher would then examine a few **FULL RECORDS** for the **relevant** books that were retrieved and notice the words/phrases that show up in the **SUBJECT** field. In this case, one couldn't help but notice these:

> **SUBJECT(S)**　　**Marijuana — Law and legislation — United States.**
> **Drug legalization — United States.**
> **Marijuana — Therapeutic use — Arizona.**

Obviously our simple 2-word search needs to be made more complex.

Taking the different useful keywords into consideration, and trying some variations out, I would end up with this fabulous search statement:

```
marijuana and (legalization or legislation or therapeutic)
```

NOW, TRY YOUR HAND at this and use OSCAR and your wits to improve each of these searches. Write your best suggestion in the space below each.

POLICE BRUTALITY works OK, but OSCAR prefers an odd word be substituted for *brutality*.

JAPANESE INTERNMENT CAMPS find something, but there is a much better way to do this.

CORPORATE CRIME works OK, but suggest a better search for this topic.

GLASS CEILING sort of works, but suggest a better search for this topic.

FIGURE 3-2

Where **exactly** will I find these?

DIRECTIONS Below are 4 citations to journal articles **found in this library**. Several different indexes/ databases were used to identify these items. That is why the citations don't all look alike. Using **OSCAR**, figure out where you would have to go next to actually put your hands on the cited items

TIP Make sure you are looking up the **journal** title (not the **article** title) on OSCAR.

TI: The evaluation of criminal responsibility: A psychobiological approach.
AU: Simon,-Robert-I.
IN: Georgetown U School of Medicine, Program in Psychiatry & Law, Washington, DC, US
JN: Psychiatric-Annals; 1992 Nov Vol 22(11) 544-546

Will it be found with   **AND would you look for it**

❑ periodicals current issues   ❑ microfiche periodicals   ❑ under the call number _____

❑ periodicals bound volumes   ❑ other location *(specify)*   ❑ alphabetically under this 1st word _____

❑ microfilm periodicals

AUTHOR:	Leef, George C
TITLE:	LAWYER FEES TOO HIGH?
JOURNAL NAME:	Regulation.
PAGES:	pp. 33
PUB DATE:	Winter 1997

Will it be found with   **AND would you look for it**

❑ periodicals current issues   ❑ microfiche periodicals   ❑ under the call number _____

❑ periodicals bound volumes   ❑ other location *(specify)*   ❑ alphabetically under this 1st word _____

❑ microfilm periodicals

Authors:	Luhmann-N
Title:	Politicians, Honesty and the Higher Amorality of Politics
Source:	THEORY CULTURE & SOCIETY 1994, Vol 11, Iss 2, pp 25-36

Will it be found with   **AND would you look for it**

❑ periodicals current issues   ❑ microfiche periodicals   ❑ under the call number _____

❑ periodicals bound volumes   ❑ other location *(specify)*   ❑ alphabetically under this 1st word _____

❑ microfilm periodicals

PAIS NO:	93-0407324
AUTHOR:	Hennelly, Michael J.
TITLE:	US policy in El Salvador: creating beauty or the beast?
JOURNAL:	(Parameters) 23:59-69 Spring 1993
PUBL TYPE:	Periodical article

Will it be found with   **AND would you look for it**

❑ periodicals current issues   ❑ microfiche periodicals   ❑ under the call number _____

❑ periodicals bound volumes   ❑ other location *(specify)*   ❑ alphabetically under this 1st word _____

❑ microfilm periodicals

FIGURE 3-3

More! I Want *More!*

Look at the book cover you have been given. Consider the topic covered. Write down some of the **key words** that describe that topic below.

You are going to be using **Expanded Academic Index** to find some **really good** articles on that topic. By **really good**, I mean articles that are more insightful than those in general newspapers and newsmagazines and less inflated by opinion than in the average commentary magazine and a lot more substantive than what you find all over the Web. It is just a matter of

  ✔ taking a little time.   ✔ looking in the right place.   ✔ looking at the right things.

Begin by connecting to Expanded Academic Index. You do this through OSCAR's **Z>Connect to Another Database** option.

Try a keyword search on your topic.

Did you get too many?

How many?
Unless you got over 1,000, just start looking at them! See **Looking!** below.

Did you get too few?

Unless you got no relevant ones at all, look at what you got very carefully! You can get some ideas for better keyword searches. See **Looking!** below.

Looking!

Do not just look at the short display list, which looks like this:

```
1  Street children around the world.   America                    Sep 97
2  Study says 180,000 homeless are d   The New York Times         Aug 97
3  There's no place called home: but   NEA Today                  Aug 97
4  What About America's Homeless Chi   Journal of Marriage and th  Jul 97
5  From marginalized to mainstreamed   Family Relations           Jul 97
```

You cannot tell much from this. The "study" article is not really the results of the study but just a short piece saying that there is a study. The 4th one is really a book review. You cannot tell which ones we have here either. So, look at the full records by selecting one, by number *(1, 2, 3, etc.)*, and then use your **F** *(for FORWARD)* option to go through them record by record.

In the full records, be sure to look at:

  ➡ how long the article is *(a number in parentheses for periodicals or in inches for NYT.)*
  ➡ the 2nd screen. You get there by typing **m** to see **MORE!** The best stuff is often on this 2nd screen.
  ➡ the subject headings! They will give you a better idea than the title of exactly what the article covers. They will also give you ideas on how to focus your search and other, even better, key words to use in searching.
  ➡ our holdings. Notice what years we have, whether any is on microform, what the call number is, what department it is in (not all are in Periodicals).
  ➡ the summary or abstract, if there is one. They can be extremely informative.

Print a few **really good** citations.

FIGURE 3-4

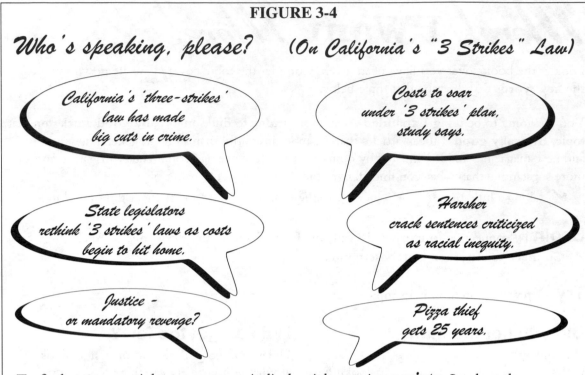

Who's speaking, please?   *(On California's "3 Strikes" Law)*

California's 'three-strikes' law has made big cuts in crime.

Costs to soar under '3 strikes' plan, study says.

State legislators rethink '3 strikes' laws as costs begin to hit home.

Harsher crack sentences criticized as racial inequity.

Justice - or mandatory revenge?

Pizza thief gets 25 years.

To find out, you might get some periodical articles, a nice **variety**. Look at the citations below. They are articles in the journals given with this sheet. ***Notice that the specific issue/page information is listed for each of the articles.*** All of these articles are about mandatory/minimum sentencing laws. For each periodical/article, answer the following questions.

➤ Start by Scanning an entire issue of each periodical, looking for things like:

✔ How often it is published?
✔ *Who* publishes/sponsors it?
✔ What kind of people write articles, especially the **FEATURE ARTICLES**.

Then, after you have a feel for the periodical, take a look at the yellow handout, ***Types of Periodicals***. Examine the categories and characteristics. Decide what type of periodical **each** is.

HINT: Each is different!

Newsweek is a _____

Washington Monthly is a _____

Crime & Delinquency is a _____

Federal Probation is a _____

FIGURE 3-4
Verso of Who's Speaking Please
(Version 1)

Finally, look for the specific articles cited below. Describe *who* you are hearing from in each particular article. I don't mean, "What is their name?" either! Rather, how do they make a living? (*Like,* CEO OF NABISCO *or* PSYCHOLOGY PROFESSOR AT STANFORD) Be as specific as you can.

AUTHOR   Bales, William D. **WHO** IS HE?_____
TITLE   Mandatory minimum sentencing in Florida: past trends and future implications.
APPEARS IN Crime and Delinquency 1992, v.38, n3, July, p309-329.

AUTHOR   Forer, Lois G. **WHO** IS SHE?_____
TITLE   Justice by the numbers.
APPEARS IN Washington Monthly 1992, v24, n4, April, p12(6).

AUTHOR   Luttrell, Mark H. **WHO** IS HE?_____
TITLE   The impact of the Sentencing Reform Act on prison management.
APPEARS IN Federal Probation 1991, v.55, n4, Dec, p54-57.

AUTHOR   Jacoby, Tamar. **WHO** IS SHE?_____
TITLE   An end to judicial roulette; similar crimes, similar crooks, similar sentences.
APPEARS IN Newsweek 1989, v113, n5, Jan 30, p76(1).

FIGURE 3-4
Verso of Who's Speaking Please
(Version 2)

Finally, look for the specific articles cited below. Describe *who* you are hearing from in each particular article. I don't mean, "What is their name?" either! Rather, how do they make a living? (*Like,* CEO OF NABISCO *or* PSYCHOLOGY PROFESSOR AT STANFORD) Be as specific as you can.

AUTHOR   Hepburn, John R. **WHO** IS HE?_____

TITLE   Organizational imperatives and sentencing reform implementation: the impact of prison practices and priorities on the attainment of the objective of determinate sentencing.

APPEARS IN Crime and Delinquency 1986, v.32, n3, July, p339-365.

AUTHOR   Bennet, James. **WHO** IS HE?_____

TITLE   Sentences that make sense; making the punishment fit the crime.

APPEARS IN Washington Monthly 1990, v21, n12, Jan, p36(12).

AUTHOR   Benekos, Peter J. **WHO** IS HE?_____

TITLE   Public policy and sentencing reform: the politics of corrections.

APPEARS IN Federal Probation 1992, v.56, n1, March, p4-10.

AUTHOR   Jacoby, Tamar. **WHO** IS SHE?_____

TITLE   Parsing the sentences; what constitutes reasonable punishment?

APPEARS IN Newsweek 1988, v112, n12, Sept 19, p82(1).

FIGURE 3-5

TYPES OF PERIODICALS

	Scholarly & Research Journals	Professional, Trade & Industry Journals	Journals of Commentary & Opinion	Newspapers	Popular Magazines
Examples	American Historical Review Journal of Educational Research Plasma Physics Social Psychology Quarterly	RN Science Teacher Restaurants and Institutions American Libraries	Mother Jones National Review Atlantic New Republic	New York Times Washington Post Christian Science Monitor Wall Street Journal	Time Newsweek Sports Illustrated Readers Digest
Values & Uses	Reports of original research; In depth analysis of issues related to the discipline; Academic level book reviews; Refereed or peer-reviewed	Current trends, news & products in a field; Company, organization, & biographical information; Statistics, forecasts; Employment & career information; Book and product reviews	Commentaries on social & political issues; Some in-depth analysis; Political viewpoints, liberal, conservative & other; Sometimes acts as voice of activist organization; Speeches & interviews; Book reviews	Current information; Hard news; Local and regional information; Classified ads; Editorials; Speeches; Book reviews; Primary source for information on events	Current events; Hot topics; Primary source for analysis of popular culture; Short articles; Generally not much depth; Interviews
Language	Academic; Can be very technical; Uses the language of the discipline	Written for practitioners; Can use jargon extensively	Written for a general educated audience	Written for a general educated audience	Non-technical language
Authors	Researchers, academics, professors, scholars, etc.	Practitioners in the field or journalists with subject expertise	Extremely variable; Can be academics, journalists, representatives of various "groups"	Journalists	Generally, journalists and freelance writers
Sources	Footnotes and bibliographies, Often very extensive documentation	Occasional brief bibliographies; Sources sometimes cited in text	Occasionally cite sources in text or provide short bibliographies	Rarely cite any sources in full	Rarely cite any sources
Publisher	Universities, scholarly presses or academic/research organizations	Commercial publishers or professional and trade associations	Commercial publishers or non-profit organizations	Commercial publishers	Commercial publishers
Graphics	Graphs, charts, formulas, depending on the discipline; No glossy ads here at all	Photographs, charts, tables, illustrations of all sorts; Sometimes glossy ads	Wide variety of appearances; Some very plain, others lots of gloss	Pictures, charts, ads of all sorts	Very glossy; Full of color ads of all sorts
Access Tools *Ask a Librarian for further details!*	*Some from Expanded Academic Index, but more from specialized indexes like Art Index, Sociological Abstracts, Religion Index, PsycLit, Communication Abstracts.*	*Business indexes like ABI-Inform or Business & Industry, or subject indexes like Education Index, Library Literature; Some the same indexes used for scholarly journals like PsycLit.*	*Expanded Academic Index; Alternative Press Index; Readers Guide; PAIS*	*National Newspaper Index; Newspaper Abstracts; Individual paper indexes*	*Expanded Academic Index; Readers Guide*

4.   Focus on Skills: Using the Classification System and Finding Periodicals

Diane Prorak
University of Idaho, Moscow, Idaho

Introduction

Basic instruction sessions often stress the online catalog and bibliographic databases while neglecting other reference sources, print indexes, and the library's classification system. To emphasize these concepts in an engaging way, the basic session can be split into two short sessions, with an independent assignment between sessions. In the first class period, students complete the worksheet that follows using a Library of Congress classification class related to their college major. They then go out into the library to find reference books, print indexes, and periodicals for that class and answer questions about the resources. Between sessions, students complete a worksheet on how to find article citations using the library's electronic indexes. The second class session reviews the concepts and skills needed to find the full article from a citation. Finally, students actually locate an article in the library and bring it back to class. This format has been received enthusiastically by both students and instructors. The format can be customized for the teaching style of the librarian, the specific assignment, the instructor's requests, or the length of the class.

Subject

Any

Level of Activity

Basic

Time Required

Preparation, 2–3 hours (first time only); one 45–60 minute class session and one 30–45 minute class session

Size of Class

Up to 40

Preparation

1. Find or prepare a basic one-page outline of the Library of Congress or Dewey Decimal Classification structure.
2. Adapt the handouts to the specific institution (first time only).
3. Copy a set of handouts for each participant. Ideally, each handout should be a different color.

Class Instructions

In the next two class sessions, we will learn about the resources available in the library and how they are organized. You will have a brief exercise between the two sessions to get personal experience with finding information on a topic of interest to you. This topic can be an area within your major, a research assignment you are working on now, or simply a topic that you would enjoy learning more about, such as a hobby or your family's ethnic background.

Throughout the sessions and the exercise, please remember that although the organization of materials in a library can be complicated, there are librarians and staff members available to help you. That includes me; please feel free to ask questions about anything concerning the library during these sessions.

Discussion

Session 1

1. Meet in the library lobby. Show students the reference section, indexes, and electronic database computers. Point out the current journals, bound journals, and newspapers. Show or explain the location of circulating books.
2. In the classroom, discuss the Library of Congress Classification (LCC) using a handout. With a transparency, briefly discuss LCC letters and parts of a call number.
3. Ask students to determine the LCC letter(s) corresponding to their major or a subject they are interested in and write the letter(s) on the worksheet entitled, "Exploring Information Sources in the Library" (Figure 4-1).
4. Before sending students out to do the worksheet, explain their task. If students have similar majors, they are encouraged to work together.
5. Students go out into the library to complete worksheets and return within about 25 minutes. Students will definitely need assistance as they work.
6. Collect completed worksheets. (Those not finished can complete them for the next class session.) Then hand out and give instructions for the worksheet, "Library Instruction: Finding Periodical Articles" (Figure 4-2). They need to complete most of this worksheet (except for the section on actually finding the article in the library) for the next class. If there is time, give a very quick demonstration of how to find articles using the library's computer system.

Session 2

1. Ask students if they had problems or questions in trying to complete the worksheet on finding articles.

2. Discuss the differences between magazines and journals. (You could bring a few magazines and journals, pass them out, and then ask students to determine whether they have a magazine or a journal. Then discuss the differences.)

3. Discuss and show the differences between current and bound issues of periodicals.

4. Review the purpose of indexes. Remind students that they looked at printed indexes when doing the first worksheet and then used an electronic index for the second worksheet.

5. Ask for a volunteer to demonstrate the article search he or she did for the worksheet and how to determine whether the library owns the periodical containing the article.

6. Discuss how periodicals are arranged (i.e., alphabetically, by LCC letters, or one way for current issues and the other for bound volumes). Ask how many found articles in periodicals that the library owned. (They should have found three article citations.) If some students found no articles in periodicals owned by the library, pair them up with someone who did. Ask students to go out into the library, find one of their articles, and bring it back to class.

7. When students return, ask them what problems they encountered. Discuss tips for finding periodicals that are not in the expected place. Discuss interlibrary loan for those articles the library does not own.

8. Collect worksheets.

FIGURE 4-1
Sample Exercise Sheet

EXPLORING INFORMATION SOURCES IN THE LIBRARY

Your name: **Date:**   **Instructor:**
Section:

Librarian:

Library of Congress Classification (LCC)

❑ Look at the LCC sheet and identify the letters that correspond to your major OR a subject area of interest and write them below:

I. Reference Books

Reference books include handbooks, dictionaries, encyclopedias, directories, almanacs, databooks, and yearbooks. The reference books are arranged alphabetically by LCC letters.

- Go to the reference books area where your LCC letters are located.
- Browse this area and try to find two reference books of interest.
- Write down the titles of the reference books you find and their call numbers below. Briefly describe what kind of information they contain.

Reference book title #1:

Call number:

Type of information in book:

Reference book title #2:

Call number:

Type of information in book:

FIGURE 4-1 cont.

II.   Indexes and Abstracts

Go to the print indexes and abstracts area. Print indexes and abstracts are arranged by LCC letters.

• Write the topic you want to investigate:_____

Using an index listed here, find an article in your subject area:

Applied Science & Technology Index	*Humanities Index*
Art Index	*Music Index*
Biological & Agricultural Index	*Physical Education Index*
Business Periodicals Index	*Social Science Index*
Education Index	

• Write down an article citation from that index:

Author:

Title of article:

Title of periodical:

Date: **Volume:**   **Page:**

III.   Periodicals (Magazines and Journals)

• Go to where the bound periodicals are shelved. Use the map in the lobby to help you locate the appropriate area. The bound periodicals are arranged by LCC letters.

• Go to the shelves where your LCC letters are located. Browse this area and look at the periodicals.

• Write down the title and call number of a periodical in your subject: _____

• Go to the shelves where current issues of magazines and journals are located. The current issues of magazines and journals are arranged alphabetically by title.

• Find the current issues of the periodical you listed in the previous step. Examine the latest issues.

• Write down a trend or topic you see in the issues that interests you: _____

IV.   Books

• Go to the floor where circulating books with your LCC letters are shelved. Find books on your topic.

• Write down the title and call number of a book you found: _____

FIGURE 4-2
Sample Periodicals Exercise Sheet

FINDING PERIODICAL ARTICLES

Your name:

Date: **Instructor:**   **Section:**

Librarian:

1. Write down the topic you will be researching for your paper, or use one of the suggestions listed below:

   Home schooling
   Internet surfing
   Endangered Species Act reauthorization
   militia groups
   fraternities/sororities
   censorship
   rafting
   computer hacking
   affirmative action in universities

   Write down other terms to narrow and describe your topic:

2. Select an index: Indexes to periodical articles can be found in both printed and electronic versions. Each index covers only a certain subject and time period. If you cannot find an article on your subject in one index, you may need to try another one.

   [Site-specific instructions for accessing electronic databases]

3. Look up your topic in the index:

   [Site-specific instructions for a basic search statement]

FIGURE 4-2 cont.

4. Print the full record (citation) for at least three articles on your topic and staple the printouts to this worksheet.

    [Site-specific instructions for displaying and printing from electronic databases]

Author:	Michael Meyer	Author of the article
Title:	Surfing the Internet in 3-D (virtual reality software on the World Wide Web)	Title of the article
Source:	Newsweek, May 15, 1995 v125 n20 p68(2)	Title of the periodical / Date, volume and article page number
Subjects:	Virtual reality - Innovations World Wide Web - Innovations	Subject words describing the article

5. Find out whether the library subscribes to these periodicals. The library does not own every periodical article included in every index. You need to search the library's catalog to find out whether the library has the periodicals for the dates on which your articles were published.

    [Site-specific instructions for identifying periodical holdings]

    *   On the printouts you created in step 4, write down the call number of each periodical (e.g., *Newsweek*).
    *   If the periodical is not in the library, write "Not in library" beside the complete title of the periodical.
    *   Repeat for each citation that you printed out.

6. Find the article in the library. (To be done during next class session.)

    Pick one of the article citations you found that the library owns.

    [Site-specific instructions for locating current, bound, and microform periodicals]

    **BRING THE PERIODICAL WITH YOUR ARTICLE
    BACK TO THE CLASSROOM**

5.   The Five-Minute Letter

Janet McNeil Hurlbert
Snowden Library, Lycoming College, Williamsport, Pennsylvania

Introduction

This brief assignment uses the writing-across-the-curriculum model, which encourages informal writing and writing as a path to clear thinking. Students assess their own learning within an instruction session and communicate this to the librarian at the end of class. A bonus is that this response may also be used as a qualitative instrument to evaluate the effectiveness of a particular class.

Subject

Any (It works especially well in first-year English courses.)

Level of Activity

Basic

Time Required

10–15 minutes

Size of Class

Any

Preparation

1. Determine what your specific goals are for an instruction session.
2. Think of questions that could be asked of students to ascertain whether these goals were met in the session.

Class Instructions

Reserve the last 10–15 minutes of class. Ask each student to write you a brief letter about their reaction to the instruction session. Give them two to three guidelines for this letter. The most general guideline might be to write about the "three knows":

1. What did you know coming into this class that was a review?
2. What did you learn today?
3. What do you still need to know to complete your class assignment?

For a more specialized class, you might ask students to address more specific areas. If you have enough time, you can request that students circle one or two ideas in their letters that they would feel comfortable sharing with the class.

Discussion

Having students prepare these letters, especially if you then ask them to share some parts of them with the class afterward, often works better than asking students if they have questions. It also brings the class together at the end in a more active way than having the librarian recap what was done or learned in the session.

In certain situations, you might want to write a letter back to the class to address some of their concerns and answer their questions. If students write their names on the letters, use their names in your response if it would not embarrass them in any way. For example, "Jane pointed out correctly that I did not provide enough information about finding authors. I will now try to elaborate."

6.   The Library Collage

Kelley McHenry and   *Jean Kent*
Seattle Central Community College   *North Seattle Community College*
Seattle, Washington   *Seattle, Washington*

Introduction

The "Library Collage" was developed to take the place of the 50-minute library tour. It is a hands-on experience that brings students into the library with their instructors to discover a diverse range of resources that directly pertain to their course of study. It introduces them to the library services and collections by requiring them to actively participate in locating materials that they will be able to use and that should appeal to their interests. It can be tailored to the specific requirements of the instructor and the research projects that the instructor has assigned.

Subject

Any

Level of Activity

Introductory/undergraduate

Time Required

50 minutes

Size of Class

12–50 students

Preparation

1. The librarian consults with the instructor to plan the orientation. During this interview, they identify the specific tools and subject areas to be covered. The librarian may elect to create a brief handout listing the tools, reference materials, and classification numbers that would be useful to the students after the session.
2. Ask the instructor to organize students into groups of 2-4 students prior to the session.
3. Produce a task sheet for each group. (See Figure 6-1.)
4. Produce a map, a basic library information handout, a brief bibliography (optional), and an evaluation form for each student.

Class Instructions

1. Please form your groups.
2. Appoint a record-keeper to document your group's progress and a time-keeper to keep you on track.
3. I have assigned each group one set of tasks. After I hand out the task sheets, please use your maps to locate the materials you have been asked to retrieve.

4. You will have 5 minutes to accomplish your tasks. Because you have only 5 minutes, I recommend that you work together rather than dividing up the tasks.
5. At the end of the 5 minutes we will meet back here in the classroom. Before you make your group reports, I will show you how I want you to present them.

Discussion

The librarian produces a set of tasks for the students to accomplish. These tasks might include using the online catalog and other computerized research tools; finding specific reference works or circulating books or selecting titles of interest from a range of call numbers; locating journal, magazine, and newspaper titles; investigating the pamphlet collection; requesting audiovisual items from the media center; etc.

Some tasks will require special arrangements. For example, if students will need to photocopy an article, arrange to have change or photocopy cards available. Not all library special collections permit materials to be taken from the room, but some are willing to make exceptions for a class exercise.

The actual orientation begins with a brief overview of the handouts and an examination of major library services. The suggested timetable follows:
10 minutes for the introduction
 5 minutes to accomplish the tasks
30 minutes for the group presentations
 5 minutes for evaluation

Each group should have 2–4 tasks to work on and should be able to complete the tasks in about 5 minutes. When the students return to the classroom, the groups take turns coming to the front of the room to report on their tasks. The librarian gives the first report to model the type of presentation desired.

Students display an interesting example of their selections or explain the purpose and use of resources that cannot be brought into the classroom. Each group is given a round of applause after its presentation.

At the end of the session, students are given an opportunity to give feedback on the process and ask questions that remain. The librarian thanks them for coming, asks them to give themselves a round of applause, and invites them to return to the library in the near future.

FIGURE 6-1
Sample Task Sheets

Go to the magazines (back issues) and select an issue of each of the following titles:

1. _____

2. _____

3. _____

Examine these publications and be prepared to briefly tell the rest of the class about them.

Go to the online catalog and look up the following SUBJECT/AUTHOR/TITLE:

_____

A step-by-step guide is located near the catalog workstations. Use it if you need help!

Be prepared to briefly tell the class the results of your search.

Go to the newspapers and select an issue of each of the following titles:

1. _____
2. _____
3. _____

Examine these publications and be prepared to briefly tell the rest of the class about them.

BRING A COPY OF EACH TITLE BACK TO THE CLASSROOM.

Go to the map file and try to understand how this collection is organized. Find a map of the following area: _____

BRING THE MAP YOU FIND BACK TO THE CLASSROOM.

Be prepared to briefly tell the rest of the class about the map file.

FIGURE 6-1 cont.

Go to the library LAN and choose the following database from the menu:
_____

Try a SUBJECT HEADING/KEYWORD search with the following term:
_____

PRINT A FEW CITATIONS OR A BRIEF ARTICLE FROM THE DATABASE.

Be prepared to briefly tell the rest of the class about the results of your search.

Go to the periodical index area and find a copy of the magazine and newspaper list.

BRING THIS LIST BACK TO THE CLASSROOM.

Be prepared to tell your classmates about this list.

Go to the pamphlet file. Find the file titled: _____

BROWSE THROUGH THE FILE AND RETURN TO CLASS WITH AN ITEM TO USE AS AN EXAMPLE.

Be prepared to share what you have learned with the class.

Go to the reference collection and browse the shelf with the following call number range:
_____

Select a book from this area that interests you and notice what other books are on the shelf nearby.

BRING THIS BOOK WITH YOU TO THE CLASSROOM.

Be prepared to share what you have learned and a little about the book you have chosen.

FIGURE 6-1 cont.

Go to the main collection and find the following book: _____

Examine the book to get an idea of what is important about it. Notice what other books are on the shelf around it.

BRING THE BOOK BACK WITH YOU TO THE CLASSROOM.

Be prepared to briefly tell the rest of the class about what you have learned as well as a little about the book you have found.

Go to the magazines (back issues).

Select an issue of the following scholarly journal(s):

1. _____

2. _____

3. _____

Select an issue of the following popular magazine(s):

1. _____

2. _____

3. _____

BRING AN ISSUE OF EACH TITLE BACK TO THE CLASSROOM.

Carefully examine these publications and be prepared to explain some of the differences among them to your classmates.

Go to the reference collection and find the following book: _____

Examine the book to get an idea of what is important about it. Notice what other books are on the shelf around it.

BRING THE BOOK BACK WITH YOU TO THE CLASSROOM.

Be prepared to briefly tell the rest of the class about what you have learned as well as a little about the book you have found.

FIGURE 6-1 cont.

Go to the main collection and find the following book: _____

Examine the book to get an idea of what is important about it. Notice what other books are on the shelf around it.

BRING THE BOOK BACK WITH YOU TO THE CLASSROOM.

Be prepared to briefly tell the rest of the class about what you have learned as well as a little about the book you have found.

Go to the microfilm collection and find the following microfilm:
_____

Take it to a microfilm reader/printer and make a copy of the first page of the article titled:
_____

BRING THE ITEM BACK WITH YOU TO THE CLASSROOM.

Be prepared to briefly tell the rest of the class about this activity.

Go to the microfiche collection and find the following microfiche:
_____

Take it to a microfiche reader/printer and make a copy of the first page of the article titled:
_____

BRING THE ITEM BACK WITH YOU TO THE CLASSROOM.

Be prepared to briefly tell the rest of the class about this activity.

Go to the reserve collection and ask for the following item:
_____

BRING THE ITEM BACK WITH YOU TO THE CLASSROOM.

Be prepared to briefly tell the rest of the class about the reserve collection and its procedures.

FIGURE 6-1 cont.

Go to the special collection and ask for the following item:

_____

BRING THE ITEM BACK WITH YOU TO THE CLASSROOM.

Be prepared to briefly tell the rest of the class about the special collection and its procedures.

Go to one of the library's LAN workstations and get a copy of the Library LAN User's Guide.

BRING THIS NOTEBOOK BACK TO THE CLASSROOM.

Be prepared to tell the class about this user's manual, how it is organized, and how to use it.

Go to the reference desk and ask the reference librarian for the following item:

_____

BRING THE ITEM BACK WITH YOU TO THE CLASSROOM.

Be prepared to briefly tell the rest of the class about the item that you have been given.

7.   Library-ese Glossary Exercise

Lisa K. Miller
Paradise Valley Community College, Phoenix, Arizona

Introduction	This is designed for use as a warm-up exercise for a basic orientation to the library. It ensures that students are familiar with the language of the library before launching into a lecture. Try as we might, there will always be some library language, or jargon, that must be used when giving instruction. This exercise is a good way to help students use this language.
	The students are given a list of questions (16) far too long for an individual to answer in 5 minutes if he or she has had no exposure to the vocabulary. However, in any group of four students in any university, one of the students will be able to answer each of the questions from previous knowledge. If not, they have the glossary sheets as a backup. Therefore, in 5 minutes the exercise gives them confidence about their previous knowledge about the library. In addition, the new terms they do pick up, they are learning from another student (perhaps a more salient source than the librarian). When the students return to listening to the orientation lecture that follows, they are energized, and they will not be distracted by new terminology.
	For best results, circulate through the room to answer questions during the discussion. State that 5 minutes will be allowed to motivate students to work quickly, but extend the exercise up to 8 minutes if students are actively discussing the terms.
Subject	Any
Level of Activity	Basic
Time Required	Preparation (first time only): 1–2 hours to adapt handouts provided below; In-class: 10 minutes
Size of Class	Up to 40 (Up to 10 groups of four students each)

Preparation

1. (First time only) Adapt the Glossary Exercise sheet (Figure 7-1) and Library-ese Glossary (Figure 7-2) as needed for your own library environment (e.g., Dewey or LC classification; any special acronyms or services).
2. Photocopy one exercise sheet and one glossary (on three separate pages) for each **group of four** in the class.
3. Photocopy the complete glossary (stapled) for each **student** in the class.

Class Instructions

So we can all become familiar with the special jargon of the library, we will now divide into groups of four for a brief exercise. (Have students count off to the number of groups needed, i.e., count to 3 for a class of 12 students; count to 10 for a class of 40 students.) Select a facilitator for your group. (Hand this person the exercise sheet, and hand the other three students in the group a different sheet of the glossary.) The facilitator will take the next 5 minutes to ask the 16 questions on the exercise sheet. Those in the group who know the term or the answer to the question can share it with the others. Use the answers on the sheets as a backup and to fill in gaps in the group's knowledge. I am here to answer any questions you have during the group discussion.

Discussion

When the exercise is completed, take back the exercise sheets and separate glossary sheets from each group. Give each student a stapled copy of the glossary to keep. Ask students to keep the glossary in the notebook they will bring into the library to refer to as needed.

Handouts for the exercise to be adapted for the individual institution follow.

FIGURE 7-1
Sample Exercise Sheet

GLOSSARY EXERCISE

As the lucky holder of this piece of paper, you will be the facilitator for your group. Take about 5 minutes and ask the questions on this sheet to your teammates. The answers will be on one of the sheets they hold. Try to get through as many of these questions as you can in the time allotted. Check off every question your teammates answer correctly.

1. Give the title of one dictionary in our library.

2. What pieces of information are included in a citation?

3. Give the title of a magazine.

4. Give the title of a journal.

5. What does LC stand for?

6. What is research?

7. What kinds of information can be found in a reference book?

8. What is the list of works cited also known as?

9. Give the titles of two popular style manuals.

10. What does CD-ROM stand for?

11. Give an example of a database.

12. What kind of help can a reference librarian give you?

13. What is meant by *call number*?

14. What can one do with an index?

15. How would you find out which periodicals a library has?

16. What database will tell you the books available in the library?

FIGURE 7-2
Sample Glossary

Library-ese Glossary

Library-ese - Strange language spoken by reference librarians and library staff. Not the native tongue of most students.

Bibliography - The list of works cited by an author at the end of an article, paper, book, or other research-based writing. There are also specialized subject bibliographies, published separately as books.

Call number - The letters and numbers assigned to a book to give it a unique location in the library. EXAMPLE: HF 5567.C45 1992

CD-ROM - Compact Disc Read Only Memory - A digitally mastered disc that holds information, usually a database.

Circulating - This means that the item may be checked out. Some Reserve items circulate only within the library.

Citation - The information given in an index or catalog about a particular title. The citation may include the article title, periodical title, book title, place of publication, publisher, volume, pages, and date. Refer to a style manual to learn how to format citations for your own bibliographies. EXAMPLES:

> BOOK: Freedman, Richard R. *What Do Unions Do?* New York: Basic, 1984.
> ARTICLE: Prince, Dinah. "Marriage in the '80s." *New York* 1 June 1987: 30–38.

Database - A collection of information, usually electronic. EXAMPLE: *Periodical Abstracts*. See the Indexes & CD-ROM Databases handout.

Dictionary - A book that gives definitions of words. Dictionaries may be general (*Webster's New Collegiate Dictionary*), or specialized (*Dictionary of Economics*).

Electronic - In libraries, this usually describes a database that can be accessed with a computer. CD-ROM and online databases are both electronic.

Encyclopedia - A compendium of information. Like dictionaries, these can be general (*Encyclopedia Britannica*) or specialized (*Encyclopedia of World Cultures*).

Index - Locates articles in periodicals by subject or author. EXAMPLES: *Social Sciences Index*; *Academic Abstracts*.

FIGURE 7-2 cont.

Journal - A periodical that is scholarly or academic in content and purpose. EX-AMPLES: *Journal of Applied Psychology* or *American Anthropologist*. Compare with magazine.

LAN - Local Area Network. This network connects computers, or workstations, allowing users to access the same databases simultaneously.

Library of Congress Classification System (LC) - The system of letters and numbers used by most academic libraries to assign a call number to materials.

Magazine - A general-interest periodical that has a broad, wide audience. EX-AMPLE: *Time* or *Glamour*. Compare with journal.

Microform - Refers to **microfiche** (rectangular) and **microfilm** (roll) formats whereby print text is transferred onto film for preservation. Usually, older issues of periodicals are transferred to microform.

Online - Refers to accessing a remote computer via a terminal. Our online catalog is one example of an online database.

Online catalog - The database that lists the books available in a given library or library district. This is the electronic equivalent of the card catalog.

OPAC - Online Public Access Catalog - Often called simply online catalog.

Pamphlet file - File cabinets holding pamphlets, brochures, clippings, etc., on a wide variety of topics. They are a vital part of the library's collection, but their formats do not allow them to be shelved with books. See the pamphlet subject headings list on top of the pamphlet file.

Periodical - A generic term for anything published periodically, including magazines, journals, and newspapers.

Periodicals list - The listing of periodicals to which a library subscribes.

Print - Ink on paper; not electronic. A book is a print resource. *Art Index* in book form is a print index.

Reference - The process of answering the questions of library patrons about research or finding information; the section of the library in which this takes place.

Reference book - A book that contains facts, statistics, biographical information, or other such as to make it a valuable tool for answering reference questions. These books may not be taken out of the library, as a rule, and are shelved separately from the rest of the collection.

FIGURE 7-2 cont.

Reference librarian - A faculty member who has studied the field of library science at the graduate level. A librarian is skilled in using <u>print</u> and <u>electronic</u> resources and is the person to ask for research assistance in the library.

Research - Diligent and thorough inquiry and investigation into a subject. This includes using ALL appropriate <u>print</u> and <u>electronic</u> sources, asking the <u>reference librarian</u> for help, and making use of <u>bibliographies</u> given by other authors.

Reserve - Where materials are placed to be used by all students in a class. Any type of material that a professor deems appropriate may be put on reserve.

Style manual - A book that tells the reader how to format a paper, with regard to footnotes, bibliographies, pagination, etc. Ask your instructor which style manual you are to use. The most commonly used style manuals are the following:

> *A Manual for Writers of Term Papers, Theses, and Dissertations* (Also called *Turabian*)

> *MLA Handbook for Writers of Research Papers*

> *Publication Manual of the American Psychological Association* (Also called *APA*)

---

8.   Modeling a Research Strategy: Horizontal and Vertical Thinking

John Riddle
West Library, College of New Jersey, (formerly Trenton State College)

Introduction

The objective of this class is to discuss research strategies for papers (10–15 pages) assigned to first-year students. For many, this is the first substantive research paper they have had to write at college. In our experience, this class is held the second semester. In the first semester, students are given an orientation to the library and an introduction to the online catalog.

This research strategy class is structured to meet the needs of students with different learning styles. Using a generalized Myers-Briggs typology, learning styles can be grouped into extroversion and introversion. One aim of the class is to reach both types of students.

The class is also designed to be as interactive as possible. Each concept is presented in 5–10 minute slots, with time allowed for students to practice the concept afterward. A final exercise brings all of the concepts together.

Subject

General rhetoric or basic English reading/writing/research course

Level of Activity

Intermediate

Time Required

One session of 75–90 minutes (given good instructor organization and facilitation skills)

Size of Class

20–25 students (However, parts can be adapted for a much larger class.)

Preparation

1. Meet or talk with class instructor to gauge the students' progress in the research process. (The class works best if topics and/or bibliographies have already been developed.) If students do not have topics, prepare samples for the class.
2. Design overhead transparencies or a Power Point presentation.
3. Collect reference tools from five distinct disciplines for the final exercise (i.e., volumes of printed indexes, one-volume encyclopedias, bibliographies.) (See Class Instructions section, below.)

4. Collect grease pencils or transparency pens, one for each group of 3–4 students in the class.

Class Instructions   In this session, the class will outline and discuss a model research strategy called "horizontal and vertical thinking." Begin by setting up two scenarios:

• Ask how many students have ever come to the library and could not find anything on their topic. (A few always nod their heads.)

• Ask how many students have ever come to the library and found too many items on their topic. (Again, a few heads nod, often the same as before.)

Suggest that when either of these scenarios occur, a warning light should go on, telling them that there is a problem with their research strategy. Suggest a simple model of thinking through the research process. (Show the model on the overhead.) **[5 minutes]**

Horizontal thinking. Horizontal thinking is simply linking key concepts of a topic statement with the word "and." Explain how students can use horizontal thinking to find what disciplines/knowledge domains might have something to say about their topic. Hand out a two-page sheet that lists the library's printed and electronic indexes by knowledge domain or discipline (e.g., anthropology, biology, chemistry).

If the students already have an approved thesis statement, they should use it. Otherwise, provide topics for the exercise. The students' first task is to use horizontal thinking to determine the key concepts of the topic as well as the knowledge domains that might yield some information. Then they are to use the handout to find at least one index for each knowledge domain they came up with. They work silently on this for about 3–4 minutes, then discuss the choices with the class. Ask volunteers to say what they found. Invariably, students will be able to come up with indexes (i.e., knowledge domains) they had not thought of before. Working privately on this exercise tends to help the introverts, who often need quiet time to think. **[10 minutes]**

Vertical thinking. Vertical thinking is simply finding related or broader terms for each of the main concepts of their thesis statement by using the word "or." If horizontal thinking tends to focus or narrow a topic, vertical thinking conversely helps to broaden their options when they conduct searches. Next, show a sample thesis statement (see Figure 8–1). Discuss the main ideas (e.g., television, children, behavior, violence), then have the students privately write down as many related or broader terms for each of the main ideas of the statements. After a few minutes, have students work in groups of 3–5 to compare notes and agree on the three best related, broader, or narrower terms for each concept. Working at first privately then in groups helps reach both the introverts and the extroverts, those who think best quietly and those who need to think out loud.

Next, ask some volunteers do a sample search on the online catalog using the vertical terms they came up with. Also have them model using both horizontal thinking and vertical thinking while searching the catalog. That is, they will combine "and" and "or" in a single search statement: television and (violence or aggress?) and children. This also leads to a fruitful discussion about the difference between keyword and subject searches. Volunteers will model finding subject headings in records they retrieved. Explain that whereas subject searches use the exact wording found in the subject heading on the screen, keywords are what they wrote on the paper in the vertical thinking exercise they did earlier. This demonstrates that keywords are their own words for concepts, and subject headings are found in the big red books (LCSH). This illustrates the fundamental difference between natural and controlled languages. **[10 minutes]**

Evaluating sources. The next step is to ask students to privately list all the ways they have used in the past to evaluate citations. Then ask the small groups to compare notes and agree on the top three things they look for when evaluating citations. Refer to an overhead that lists the major points (date, title, length, bibliography, credentials of the author or journal, etc.—see Figure 8–2). This helps to reinforce their points as well as to cover ones they might have missed. **[10 minutes]**

Integrating exercise. A final exercise pulls together everything discussed in the session using the model thesis statement presented earlier. (Does violence on television have damaging effect on the behavior or attitudes of young children?) Reference tools for this thesis statement might include the following:
- *Communication Abstracts*
- *Encyclopedia of Early Childhood Education*
- *Mass Media Bibliography*
- *Psychological Abstracts*

- *Social Sciences Index*

These are all print sources, but there is no reason why an electronic source could not be used if available in the classroom.

Give each small group a reference tool and assign them the following tasks:

1. Appoint a recorder to fill out an overhead template (see Figure 8-3).
2. Appoint a presenter to make a class presentation.
3. The group will examine citations in the reference tool pertaining to the thesis statement.
4. The groups will select three citations and justify them using the evaluative criteria discussed earlier.
5. The recorder will write on the transparency template the title of the reference tool used, the citations (not necessarily in MLA format), why they chose them, and how they evaluated the citations.
6. The presenter will explain to the class what the group selected and why.

[30–40 minutes]

Conclude by noting that the one thesis statement led to valuable sources from five separate knowledge domains (sociology, communications, media, psychology, and education). Using the horizontal thinking and vertical thinking model can help them do the same for their topics. **[5 minutes]**

Discussion

Each group should have 3–5 students. The final exercise requires at least three members, but if there are more than five, some members might not be able to participate fully. Be sure to structure the task explicitly so students focus immediately on what to do.

The key to completing the activity in one session is to limit the class to three or four main concepts. If time is short, the third topic, evaluating sources, can simply be discussed without engaging in an exercise. The exercises will provide practice with each concept that reach both introverts and extroverts. Be well organized and keep an eye on the time. Times shown in the class instructions are averages, so be flexible. If a particular exercise yields good discussion or lots of questions, stay with it and reduce a later exercise. However, allow plenty of time for the final exercise, which is not only the most fun for students, but also effectively pulls together everything discussed in the class.

FIGURE 8-1
Sample Topic Transparency

DOES VIOLENCE ON TELEVISION HAVE A DAMAGING EFFECT ON THE BEHAVIOR AND ATTITUDE OF YOUNG CHILDREN?

FIGURE 8-2
Evaluating Sources Transparency

EVALUATING RESOURCES/CITATIONS

How do you know which of the sources you find might be the most appropriate for your topic?

$$Million Dollar Question$$

Guideposts:

1. Abstract - in periodical index or at beginning of article

2. Title of article/journal

3. Date of publication

4. Length of article

5. Footnotes/bibliography

6. Author's credentials

Read it!!! (Or at least skim it.)

FIGURE 8-3
Integrating Exercise Transparency

HORIZONTAL AND VERTICAL THINKING

	AND	AND	AND
OR			
OR			
OR			

9. The Rhythm of Research

Gabriela Sonntag
California State University-San Marcos

Introduction

Students are introduced to the steps in the research process, beginning with music and working through the use of maps, videos, and texts. Students work in small groups to respond to a research question. After the library experience, students will:

• Have a clearer idea of the research process, including developing a research question, gathering information from various library sources, taking notes, and citing sources.

• Understand that information on a topic can be gathered from different types of material in the library (compact discs, audiocassettes, videotapes, maps, books).

The learning process in the class consists of the following steps:

1. Listen to three audio recordings.
2. Discuss similarities and differences.
3. Develop a research question.
4. Investigate answers to the question in various sources.
5. Develop a more complex research question.
6. Support their conclusion with further evidence.
7. Cite sources where evidence was obtained and where more on the subject can be found.

Subject

General interest, including music, dance, art, history (African diaspora), ethnic studies, Latin American studies

Level of Activity

Basic

Time Required

Selecting and previewing the materials to be used: 2–3 hours (first time only)
Preparation for each class: about 1 hour
Time in class: Minimum of 50 minutes

Size of Class

Any

Preparation

1. Select and preview music from Africa and Cuba. (See suggestions, below.)
2. Gather appropriate reference books (annuals, encyclopedias, almanacs, atlases, etc.). (See suggestions, below.)
3. Find a large wall map to bring to class.
4. Prepare the worksheet (see Figure 9-1).

Class Instructions

Introduce the session by explaining the value of learning research skills early in college and describing the goals of the session. **[5 minutes]**

Explain that the sample research process for the class will begin with listening to music. Remind students that listening well is very important to success in college. Play a selection of African music (e.g., *African Songs and Rhythms for Children*, selection 2 on side A). Ask students what they are hearing and write their responses on the board or flip chart (clapping, drums, chanting, singing, beat, rhythm, etc.) Ask them what type of music this is.

Next, play a selection of Cuban music (e.g., *Cuba: Afro-Cuban Songs and Rhythms*, selection 5). Again, ask students to name what they are hearing and write their ideas on the board. Ask them what type of music this is. Someone might suggest Mexican music because the lyrics are in Spanish. If so, play a selection of Mariachi music to compare the features.

Replay the Cuban music. If no one guesses correctly within a reasonable time, tell students that the music is from Cuba, in the Caribbean. Ask a student to show where Cuba and Africa are located on a map. Explain that the sample research question is, "Why are African and Cuban music so similar?"

Form groups of 4-5 students each and pass out worksheets to each student. They will review the selected reference books for information to answer the question. Have them fill out the worksheet and write the answer in their own words. Allow about 10 minutes. Ask students why it is important to write down the title, author, and page number where they found information in each book. Discuss briefly the importance of citing sources and of having a bibliography or list of sources used. Walk among the groups to answer questions. Next, have the groups report back about what they discovered, allowing 2-3 minutes per group.

To reinforce the students' research, show the video on Cuba (from Spectrum Associates) and the *Routes of Rhythm* video (the section on Indians, the need for a labor force, Africans on ships, and the master drummer). The students should understand that these videos are also part of the research and reinforce what they found in the books. They could do further research into dance, art, the Yoruba tribes of West Africa, or much more.

Wrap up by asking for questions and then refining the original, very simplistic, research question, discussing the sources of information and the types of information found in each source. Wrap up by asking for questions.

Discussion

This activity has been done with various age groups, with slight modification, from grade 4 through first-year college students. The use of children's books as sources makes the activity fun (not too taxing) and gets the point across to all groups. Ideally, if there is sufficient time, the students would do a second worksheet in the library and come back to report to the class what they found in the online catalog and in additional sources. Each group would work on a separate area: LC subject headings, printed indexes, electronic indexes, Internet sources, bibliographies, etc.

SUGGESTED VIDEOS AND AUDIOTAPES

Africa: Drum, Chant & Instrumental Music (sound recording). New York: Elektra/Nonesuch, 1988, 1976.

Amoaku, W. K. *African Songs and Rhythms for Children* (sound recording). Washington, D.C.: Smithsonian/Folkways. Nationally distributed by Rounder Records, 1989.

Cuba: Afro-Cuban Songs and Rhythms (sound recording). Paris: Arion, 1988.

Cuba (videorecording). Produced and directed by George Pitt. Spectrum Associates, 1990.

Routes of Rhythm (videorecording). Produced and directed by Eugene Rosow and Howard Dratch; written by Linda Post, Eugene Rosow, and Howard Dratch. Presented by Harry Belafonte. Santa Monica, Calif.: Cultural Research & Communication, 1989.

Sounds of West Africa: The Kora and the Xylophone (sound recording). New York: Lyrichord, 198-.

SUGGESTED REFERENCE BOOKS

Crouch, Clifford W. *Cuba*. New York: Chelsea House, 1991. ISBN 0791013626

Cultural Atlas of Africa. Ed. Jocelyn Murray. New York: Facts on File, 1981. ISBN 0871965585

Fairfield, Sheila. *Peoples and Nations of Africa: A Short History of Each Country of Africa*. Milwaukee: Gareth Stevens Pub., 1988. ISBN 1555329039

Griffiths, John. *The Caribbean*. New York: Bookwright Press, 1989. ISBN 0531182746

Holland, Gini. *Cuba Is My Home*. Milwaukee, Wis.: Gareth Stevens Pub., 1992. ISBN 0836808487

Kreikemeier, Gregory Scott. *Come with Me to Africa: A Photographic Journey*. Racine, Wis.: Western Publishing, 1993. ISBN 0307656608

Lindop, Edmund. *Cuba*. New York: Watts, 1980. ISBN 0531041018

Meltzer, Milton. *Slavery: A World History*. 1st Da Capo Press ed. New York: Da Capo, 1993. ISBN 0306805367

Suchlicki, Jaime. *Cuba: From Columbus to Castro*. 3rd ed., rev. Washington: Brassey's (US), 1990. ISBN 0080374506

Wright, David. *The Facts on File Children's Atlas*. New York: Facts on File, 1993. ISBN 0816029253

FIGURE 9-1

RESEARCH PROCESS WORKSHEET

1. Pick a topic for your research: music, Africa, Cuba

2. Look up your topic in the index or table of contents. (Some books might not be very helpful!)

3. Write one or two sentences, in your own words, on what you found and how it relates to the research question.

4. Note the citation information about the book you used:

   Author or editor (if applicable):

   Title:

   Publisher:

   Date: **Volume:**

   Pages where information on this topic can be found:

10. Structuring a Session with Questions

Lori Mestre
W. E. B. Du Bois Library, University of Massachusetts Amherst

Introduction

This activity can be used in classes of any level or subject focus as a way of creating a session according to the expressed needs of the class. It generates enthusiasm and teaches students that interaction with librarians is very productive. Students seem to have a better grasp of the material and retain the information longer because they had a hand in structuring the presentation.

By asking questions, students feel validated and are tuned in for more active listening because they are interested in the answers to their own questions. In addition, students who are asked to participate early in a session are more likely to continue participating.

Subject

Any

Level of Activity

Basic, intermediate, or advanced concepts

Time Required

50 minutes to 3 hours

Size of Class

Up to 25

Preparation

Have available a large chalk/marker board or several flip charts.

Class Instructions

There is a broad range of library expertise among the people in this room—some of you might never have used an academic library before, and others might feel very comfortable doing research. Regardless of our background, we can all learn a lot by talking to one another. Today's session will be tailored to the questions you have about how the library is organized and the services that are offered here.

In the next 3 minutes, you will pair off and write down three questions you would like to have answered during the session. I will write your questions on the board, and then we will discuss the answers and share our experiences with the best ways of using the library.

Discussion

As the pairs of students discuss their questions, they are often able to provide answers or a tip for each other's suggested questions. This generally eliminates the very basic questions and allows the more complex questions to surface. Students often start out with a basic question, but, after talking with someone, they realize they have additional questions that did not occur to them before.

After 3 minutes of discussion in pairs, go around the room and ask students to read their questions. Write them on the board or flip chart, sorting them as you go into broad areas (e.g., general information, technology, finding articles). Usually after half the pairs have reported, some of the questions have already been asked, so it does not take long to go through the group. When all of the pairs' questions are on the board, ask whether there are additional questions that have occurred to someone during the reporting process.

Start with the first set of questions and ask the group whether anyone knows the answer based on previous research in the library. This generates valuable feedback about students' real experiences in the library and reveals any misconceptions about the research process or library procedures.

Reinforce, tactfully correct, or expand on students' ideas, using computer demonstrations to illustrate points as appropriate. These demonstrations can be done by the librarian or by a student with coaching from the class. In this way, the group must get involved, use the correct terminology, and read the information on the screen carefully. Students' tips are generally received eagerly by other students.

As the discussion progresses, check the questions off the board so no questions are forgotten. If there are questions that cannot be answered in the session, arrange to follow up with the instructor or with individual students. This continues the interaction beyond the class session and reinforces the library's interest in students' successful research.

11. Dewey and the Book Covers

Christine Drew
St. Norbert College Library, De Pere, Wisconsin

Introduction	This exercise introduces students to the Dewey Decimal Classification (DDC) system.
Subject	Education (The exercise can be adapted to many disciplines.)
Level of Activity	Basic
Time Required	10 minute lecture; 10 minutes for students to complete exercise; 2 minutes per student to report
Size of Class	Maximum of 25 students
Preparation	1. Procure book covers and select ones with catchy titles that would be easy to classify in the 100 divisions of Dewey, or even further into the Education classification. 2. Duplicate copies of the DDC. 3. Duplicate copies of the Education DDC or prepare an outline of the Dewey classification for your field.
Class Instructions	1. Give a 10-minute lecture on the general DDC breakdown by hundreds, then under Education (or your subject). 2. Distribute a book cover to every student.
Discussion	Each student must identify the general classification number for his or her book. A few can be very specific, such as *Handbook of Research on Curriculum*, so that the students can even break down to the 375 level (or other area of the classification) using their handouts as a guide. They each must state their title to the class and give the 100 division (or more precise classification number) that the book would be in.

12. What's My (Subject) Line? Or, You Can't Always Judge a Subject by Its Book Cover!

Janice A. Sauer
University of South Alabama, Mobile, Alabama

Introduction

This active learning exercise has proven to be extremely effective in alerting students to the difference between
Library of Congress Subject Heading searching and keyword searching on an online catalog. The book cover quiz provides a realistic and tangible lead-in to an explanation of the difficulties and the benefits of using a controlled vocabulary.

Level of Activity

Basic

Time Required

Adjustable

Size of Class

Class needs to be small enough for students to feel comfortable volunteering answers. It can also be adapted to a small-group activity.

Preparation

1. Identify the source for obtaining discarded book jackets in your library.
2. Select book jackets that are about obvious subjects but have obscure, dated, or convoluted LC subject headings. Titles like *Complying with the ADA, Reengineering the Corporation, Justices of the Supreme Court*, or *Factory Farming* work quite well.

Class Instructions

3. Print out the full form of each bibliographic record and tape each one to the inside of the appropriate book cover. For a small group exercise, tape the covers shut.

Discussion

Hold up an individual book cover. Have the students tell you aloud how they might find this particular book using a subject search. Allow plenty of time for them to think about what words they might use to retrieve the record for this item. Continue taking answers until you have a good variety of words that could be used. Then tell them the LC subject headings required to retrieve the record. For small groups, distribute covers, allow time for discussion, and have a recorder report words chosen for each item. Then have them remove the tape and read the subject headings.

This is a perfect lead-in to the usefulness of both the big red books and keyword searching. If a computer is available in the classroom, demonstrate the use of keyword searching to find the LC subject headings. Then search on some of the subject headings and look at other titles that can be retrieved by using them.

13. Question Analysis for Autobiography

Randy Burke Hensley
University of Hawai'i at Manoa
Honolulu, Hawai'i

Elizabeth Hanson
Indiana University
Bloomington, Indiana

Introduction

Based on the analogy of human memory as a database, this exercise seeks to teach students how to develop a controlled vocabulary appropriate to the database in hand by constructing one for an autobiography. It establishes the basics of information seeking in the library by thus introducing the concepts important to constructing a controlled vocabulary.

Subject

Writing courses; freshman/new student orientation

Level of Activity

Basic

Time Required

Preparation: photocopying time; in-class: 30 minutes

Size of Class

Any number is fine; break class up into groups of two or three.

Preparation

Prepare a handout delineating the four parts of the question analysis process (Figure 13-1).

Discussion

The students are given an assignment to write a three-page autobiography. This assignment is approached by presenting the metaphor of memory as database. In order to retrieve information from this "database" effectively, the student needs a search strategy that matches the structure of the database and the application for the information. The search strategy taught is based on Cerise Oberman's writing. The question analysis form is comprised of four parts or steps:

Keywords: Key concepts or events about the student's life and what they want to say about them

Synonyms: Alternative names or words for these key concepts (e.g., nicknames or the proper names of things like their churches or schools or clubs)

Narrow terms: Aspects of the key concepts of their lives; special stories that illustrate the importance of church or family, specific events, or a particular day in their life that was significant

Broader terms: What is the larger significance of their life; what does it all mean or relate to, such as how a student's family influenced their decision to go to college

After the explanation, the students are given a sheet of paper with the four steps of question analysis and are allocated 20 minutes to work in groups of two or three to complete the sheet. The instructors roam among the groups providing guidance and clarification.

Not only does this process give the students a structure for their writing assignment, but it also establishes the basics of information seeking in the library by introducing the concepts necessary to construct a controlled vocabulary.

FIGURE 13-1
Question Analysis Process Handout

Ask yourself some questions about the information you want to find in order to make a list of words to use in the library's computers:

KEYWORDS (What are the main words that describe your subject and what you want to say about it?)
SYNONYMS (What other words can you use that mean the same thing as your Keywords?)

NARROWER TERMS
(What are some specific things you want to know about your Keywords or Synonyms?)
 	
   TIME:
   GEOGRAPHY:
   POPULATION:

BROADER TERMS: (What larger subjects include your Keywords or Synonyms?)

Section II

Searching Indexes and Online Catalogs

Edited by William Orme and Kevin M. Roddy

A variety of print, CD-ROM and remote periodical indexes vie for a student's attention in today's college and university libraries. Unfortunately, the seductive nature of searching for information by computer has convinced many students that online information is superior to that found in print. Often, students will abandon engaging research topics for lack of information found readily online.

Most of today's college students were exposed to print indexes like *Readers' Guide* before attending college (whether they remember them or not!). Some students remembered periodical print indexes, and often familiarized themselves with other types of print indexes, such as local and national newspaper indexes. Librarians must *constantly* remind students of the wealth of information found in print, and to always supplement online information with print information.

The active learning exercises in this chapter use both print and online indexes, often comparing and evaluating the two. The exercises are designed for use in an electronic classroom, but can be used near the library's terminals. Using these exercises, librarians can abandon a passive "demo" lecture. Students become more active in the learning process, master course content connected to an assignment, learn the mechanical and intuitive skills needed to navigate in an information-rich world. The exercises offer opportunities to break barriers that have isolated students and inhibited the growth of community. Collaboration offers dynamic ways to re-energize "stale" sessions, allowing librarians to participate more fully in the teaching experience.

The exercises can also be adapted to "print index only" environments; in fact, we encourage librarians to include exercises using print indexes. The Hawaiians are fond of reminding their children "Aohe pau ka ike i ka halau hookahi"—'All knowledge is not found in one place.' Today's students must remember this as well.

14. Understanding Print and Electronic Indexes

Shelle Witten and Lisa K. Miller
Paradise Valley Community College, Phoenix, Arizona

Introduction	Groups of students are given the task of comparing and contrasting the features of print and electronic indexes. Each group examines a particular print or electronic source using a research topic. Topics may be assigned or chosen by group members. Each group member is assigned a particular task to help meet the group's overall objective.
Subject	Any
Level of Activity	Basic
Time Required	Preparation—20 minutes; in-class—30 minutes
Size of Class	Maximum of 40 students (10 groups of 4)
Preparation	1. Make copies of library exercise worksheet (Figure 14-1), one for each group.
	2. Collate four copies of the Indexes and Databases handout (Figure 14-2) with one copy of the worksheet.
Class Instructions	1. Divide the class into groups of four and distribute the collated exercises with handouts to each group.
	2. Each group member is assigned a task within the group (Figure 14-3). The Navigator steers the group to the indexes; the Helmsman opens the print index or does the keyboarding; the Recorder fills in the worksheet; and the Reporter gives a one-minute presentation on what the group did.
	3. Have groups select a topic or assign one.
	4. Search your topic and return to your seats in 15 minutes. (Don't forget which responsibility you have within your group!)
	5. Groups share results with the entire class. Reporting results is the key part of this exercise. I would encourage librarians to steer this discussion away from the index as an artifact and toward the kinds of information found in it. The report template has been built into the attached exercise aid.

FIGURE 14-1

NAMES _____
INSTRUCTOR_____
CLASS _____
SECTION _____

LIBRARY EXERCISE

1. Form groups of four around common broad topics such as: Assisted Suicide; Violence on Television; Homelessness; Gangs; Elections; Water Conservation; College Athletes and Grades; or a topic chosen by your group: _____ (fill in blank, or circle topic chosen).

   As a group, you must help your reporter prepare a one-minute report. By filling in the template, number 5 on the back of this sheet, you will have an outline for your report. Do this only after you have completed exercises 2, 3, and 4.

2. Using the Indexes and Databases handout, select **one** appropriate **print index** and one **database**. Fill in the title of each resource in the appropriate blanks for numbers 3 and 4 below.

   Title of **Print** Index _____(Do **NOT** choose *Readers' Guide*)

   Title of **Database** _____

3. Using one of the current volumes of the print index selected, fill in the following:

a. What were useful **subject heading(s)** for your topic? _____

b. What, if any, were some useful **subheading(s)**? These are the headings that help narrow a major subject heading. (They are the centered headings following the major heading.) _____

c. What, if any, are some of the **related** subject headings? (These are the *see also* subject headings listed immediately following a major subject heading.)

   _____

d. Look through the list of articles following the subject heading. If possible, select an article from a periodical to which the library subscribes.

   _____

FIGURE 14-1 cont.

Give the citation for the article, as follows:

Title of article _____

Author's name _____

Title of journal _____

Date of journal issue _____Page numbers _____

Does the library subscribe to this periodical, or is it available in full text on InfoTrac?
❑ Subscribe   ❑ Don't subscribe   ❑ Available in full text on InfoTrac

If the library subscribes to this periodical, where would you find the article?
❑ Periodical back issues shelves   ❑ Microfilm

If necessary, would you be able to make a copy?   ❑ Yes ❑ No

4. Title of *database* selected _____
a. What is/are the search term(s) you used to find items on your subject?

b. Did this database have only citations to articles? Or does it have only the entire text of
   the articles? Or does it have only citations with abstracts (summaries of articles)? Or
   does this database have a combination of all of the above?

c. Select one article or document that, judging from the title, and perhaps the abstract,
   appears to be useful in your research.

Give the citation for the article or document, as follows:
Title of article _____
Author's name _____

Title of journal/newspaper/magazine/document_____
Date of issue_____Page numbers _____

d. Is the full text available in the database? _____
   If not, does the library subscribe to the periodical? _____(ERIC documents) (Use the
   library's periodical holdings list.)

FIGURE 14–1 cont.

5. **Report Template:**
a. Topic researched: _____

b. Title of print index used: _____

c. Title of database used: _____

d. Describe how these two sources *differ*._____

e. Describe how these two sources are *similar*._____

f. Which source gives *only citations* to journal articles? _____

g. Which source provides a combination of citations, abstracts, and the full text of magazine and journal articles or documents? _____

h. If you are required to use scholarly journals in your research, which source would most successfully fulfill this requirement? Why?

i. Would one of these sources give access to popular magazines? If so, which one?

FIGURE 14-2

INDEXES AND DATABASES

The library has several different tools to access the contents of periodicals and other sources. This lists them for you and tells you the purpose of each tool.

FINDING ARTICLES
1. Select the indexes or databases that best suit your topic.
2. Search them, using your subject headings or keywords.
3. Write down or print the citation (some databases give full text).
4. Locate one of the library's periodical holdings lists.
5. Look up the title of the periodical in the notebook.
6. Note whether that issue is in paper, microform, or on InfoTrac:
   a. Paper issues are stored on the shelves in the northeast corner.
   b. Microforms are in the cabinets near the Information Desk.
   c. InfoTrac is accessible on any computer in the library.
7. Retrieve that issue.
8. If not here, fill out an interlibrary loan form.

PRINT INDEXES

ART INDEX
A. Architecture, art history, fine arts, photography, films, and related fields
B. 1982–present
C. Art journals
D. Subject and author

BIOGRAPHY INDEX
A. Biographical material
B. 1982–1993
C. Magazines and books
D. Subject; also index of people by occupation

BUSINESS PERIODICALS INDEX
A. Accounting, marketing, banking, computer technology, economics, finance and investments, management, public relations, and other businesses and industries
B. Current 10 years
C. Business magazines and journals
D. Subject and author

~~~~~~~~~~~~~~~~~~~~~~~~~~KEY~~~~~~~~~~~~~~~~~~~~~~~~~

A. Subjects covered by the source   C. Types of materials indexed
B. Dates of index owned by the library   D. Ways to search for articles in the index

~~~~~~

FIGURE 14-2 cont.

EDUCATION INDEX

A. Education, preschool through adult
B. Current 10 years
C. Education magazines and journals
D. Subject and author

GENERAL SCIENCE INDEX

A. Astronomy, biology, chemistry, earth science, environment, food and nutrition, genetics, medicine, microbiology, oceanography, physics, and zoology
B. Current 10 years
C. Science magazines and journals
D. Subject and author

HUMANITIES INDEX

A. Archaeology and classical studies, area studies, film, folklore, history, language and literature, performing arts, philosophy, religion, theology, and related subjects
B. 1982–present
C. Humanities journals
D. Subject and author

READERS' GUIDE TO PERIODICAL LITERATURE

A. General interest–all subjects
B. 1900–present
C. Popular interest and news magazines
D. Subject and author

SOCIAL SCIENCES INDEX

A. Anthropology, economics, geography, law and criminology, public administration, political science, psychology, social aspects of medicine, sociology, and related subjects
B. Current 10 years
C. Social science magazines and journals
D. Subject and author

~~~~~~~~~~~~~~~~~~~~KEY~~~~~~~~~~~~~~~~~~~~

A. Subjects covered by the source   C. Types of materials indexed
B. Dates of index owned by the library   D. Ways to search for articles in the index

FIGURE 14-2 cont.

DATABASES
(CD-ROM unless otherwise noted)

ACADEMIC ABSTRACTS (Some full text)
A. General subjects
B. 1984–present
C. 800+ magazine and journal titles, 130 of which are full text
D. Subject, name, periodical title, date, keyword

BUSINESS DATELINE (Full text)
A. Any business-related subject covered in regional newspapers
B. 1985–present
C. Business sections of major city newspapers and regional business journals
D. Subject, geographical area, company name, personal name, SIC code, etc.

CD SOURCEBOOK OF AMERICAN HISTORY (Full text)
A. Key events in American history
B. Historical
C. Key documents, chapters from books, biographical information
D. Subject, keyword, name

COLLEGESOURCE (College catalogs) (Full text)
A. Catalogs of U.S. colleges
B. Current editions
C. College catalogs
D. School name, tuition, degree, enrollment, affiliation, state

ENCARTA ENCYCLOPEDIA (Full text)
A. Multimedia encyclopedia
B. Historical
C. Compendium of knowledge
D. Subject, keyword, name, etc.

~~~~~~~~~~~~~~~~~~~~~~~~~~~~~~~~~KEY~~~~~~~~~~~~~~~~~~~~~~~~~~~~~~~

A. Subjects covered by the source   C. Types of materials indexed
B. Dates of index owned by the library   D. Ways to search for articles in the index
~~~~~~

FIGURE 14-2 cont.

ERIC (Educational Resources Information Center)
A. Education, preschool through adult
B. 1966–present
C. Contains abstracts of more than 200,000 published and unpublished documents and journal articles, including evaluations, reports, surveys, guides, position papers, instructional and resource materials
D. Subject, author, journal title, language, date, etc.

EXPANDED ACADEMIC INDEX ASAP (InfoTrac) (Online database)
(Accessible via the online catalog, LAN, or the Web)
A. General interest–all subjects
B. 1992–present
C. Journal and magazine citations with summaries and some full text
D. Subject, title, author, and keyword

GALE'S LITERARY INDEX
A. Literary criticism and biographical information on authors
B. Current
C. A master index to 32 literary series published by Gale Research; combines and cross-references more than 110,000 author names and 120,000 titles
D. Title, author, nationality, date

JOURNAL OF THE AMERICAN CHEMICAL SOCIETY (Full text)
A. Chemistry
B. 1995–
C. Full text of this journal
D. Issue, subject, keyword, author

NATIONAL TRADE DATA BANK (Full text)
A. International trade, import/export, global business
B. Current year
C. Government documents
D. Subject, agency, program, document titles

~~~~~~~~~~~~~~~~~~~~~~~~~~~~~~~~~~~KEY~~~~~~~~~~~~~~~~~~~~~~~~~~~~~

A. Subjects covered by the source   C. Types of materials indexed
B. Dates of index owned by the library   D. Ways to search for articles in the index

FIGURE 14-2 cont.

NEW YORK TIMES (Full text)
A. All the news that's fit to print
B. 1991–present
C. Daily newspaper
D. Subject, name, date, title words

NEWSFILE (Formerly called *CD NEWSBANK*) (Full text)
A. Topics currently in the news
B. 1993–present
C. Selected newspaper articles as well as feature newswire service articles
D. Keyword/subject with ability to limit by date, location, etc.

SIRS (Social Issues Resource Series) (Full text)
A. Social issues, global events, and science topics
B. 1989–present
C. Magazines, newspapers, reference sources
D. Subject and keyword

SIRS GOVERNMENT REPORTER (Full text)
A. Current events, social issues, science, politics, education, etc.
B. Current
C. Government documents
D. Subject and agency

SIRS RENAISSANCE (Full text)
A. Literature, music, performing arts, philosophy, religion
B. Current year
C. Magazines and humanities journals
D. Subject headings, keywords, award recipients

Please ask a librarian if you need help using these or other resources.

~~~~~~~~~~~~~~~~~~~~~~~~~~~~KEY~~~~~~~~~~~~~~~~~~~~~~~~~~~~

A. Subjects covered by the source   C. Types of materials indexed
B. Dates of index owned by the library   D. Ways to search for articles in the index
~~~~~~

FIGURE 14-3

GROUP MEMBER TASKS

1. NAVIGATOR
Find the index, guide the group in its use.

2. HELMSMAN
Turn the pages or type at the keyboard.

3. RECORDER
Write down the citation and complete the worksheet.

4. REPORTER

Give a one-minute report to the class on what your group did.

15. Introduction to the Online Catalog and Periodical Databases

Gale Burrow
Claremont Colleges, Claremont, California

Introduction	This exercise provides first-year students with a guided introduction to the basics of searching the online catalog and subject-specific library databases. Questions in the exercises were designed to draw students' attention to results as well as allow for hands-on experience. Include more questions of an evaluative nature on the worksheets if time warrants.
Subject	Any
Level of Activity	Basic
Time Required	45–50 minutes
Size of Class	15, divided into groups of two or three

Preparation

1. Schedule the session, review databases and search topics with professor, and decide what aspects of searching need to be taught.
2. Develop search examples, exercises, and review with professor.
3. Photocopy the "Practice with Library Databases" exercise sheet (Figure 15-1) and send to professor. Ask that students be arranged into groups prior to the session. These exercises can be supplemented with questions that require students to retrieve items from the periodical and book stacks.

Class Instructions

1. Begin the active learning session with a demonstration of the online catalog. Do author, title, and subject searches. **[5 minutes]**
2. Distribute exercise sheets to each group, and have students work together to complete the exercises using the online catalog. **[10 minutes]**
3. While students are searching, circulate and assist groups as needed.
4. Reconvene and ask what students learned. **[5 minutes]**
5. Instruct students on how to formulate search statements for periodical databases. Talk about how various databases require different search strategies. Tell the class which databases each group will be searching. **[5 minutes]**

6. Have students work on the second activity. Allot ten minutes for completion.

7. Reconvene, discuss what students learned about periodical databases, and then discuss similarities and differences among the various databases and between the online catalog and the periodical database.

FIGURE 15-1
Practice with Library Databases

Set 1
Online Catalog
Online computer catalogs identify the books and periodicals (journals, magazines, newspapers) owned by the library.

You **cannot** use the online catalog to search for articles in periodicals.

1. How many books **by** David Hume do you find?

2. How many copies do you find of Hume's *Dialogues Concerning Natural Religion*?

3. How many entries do you find **about** Hume?

4. Are any of those books specifically about *Dialogues Concerning Natural Religion*?

5. What other authors have written on the subject of natural religion?

6. Were any of those authors contemporaries of Hume (1711-1776)?

CD-ROM: Expanded Academic Index (EAI)
EAI indexes articles in periodicals, including both scholarly journals and popular magazines, and covers all subject areas. It only includes periodicals published in English, mostly in the United States, in the last several years.

1. Find entries (citations to articles in periodicals) on David Hume.

2. If you find more than 10 entries, limit the search to retrieve fewer entries on a more specific subject. For example, find only those entries on Hume which also concern religion or natural religion. (Try not to limit your search to too few articles.)

3. Find entries on natural religion.

4. Looking at the entries you found, what other philosophers have written on natural religion?

5. What other subjects in EAI are related to the idea of natural religion?

6. Select an interesting entry and print the full record (including the abstract if there is one). Is the article available in our libraries?

FIGURE 15-1 cont.

Set 2
Online Catalog
Online computer catalogs identify the books and periodicals (journals, magazines, newspapers) owned by the library.

You **cannot** use the online catalog to search for articles in periodicals.

1. How many books **by** David Hume do you find?

2. How many copies do you find of Hume's *Dialogues Concerning Natural Religion*?

3. How many entries do you find **about** Hume?

4. Are any of those books specifically about *Dialogues Concerning Natural Religion*?

5. What other authors have written on the subject of natural religion?

6. Were any of those authors contemporaries of Hume (1711-1776)?

CD-ROM: Periodical Contents Index (PCI)
PCI indexes articles in North American scholarly journals from 1900 to 1960. It includes journals in the humanities and social sciences (no sciences).

1. Find entries (citations to articles in periodicals) on David Hume.

2. If you find more than 10 entries, limit the search to retrieve fewer entries on a more specific subject. For example, find only those entries on Hume which also concern religion or natural religion. (Try not to limit your search to too few articles.)

3. Find entries on natural religion.

4. Looking at the entries you found, who besides Hume has written on natural religion?

5. Select an interesting entry and print it. Is the article available in our libraries?

FIGURE 15-1 cont.

Set 3
Online Catalogs

Online computer catalogs identify the books and periodicals (journals, magazines, newspapers) owned by the library.

You **cannot** use the online catalog to search for articles in periodicals.

1. How many books **by** David Hume do you find?

2. How many copies do you find of Hume's *Dialogues Concerning Natural Religion*?

3. How many entries do you find **about** Hume?

4. Are any of those books specifically about *Dialogues Concerning Natural Religion*?

5. What other authors have written on the subject of natural religion?

6. Were any of those authors contemporaries of Hume (1711-1776)?

CD-ROM: MLA Bibliography
MLA is an international index to scholarly literature in the fields of literature, languages, linguistics, and folklore. It includes articles in journals, articles (essays) in book, books, and dissertations. The CD-ROM covers from 1981 to the present.

1. Find entries (citation to articles, book, etc.) on David Hume.

2. If you find more that 10 entries, limit the search to retrieve fewer entries on a more specific subject. For example, find only those entries on Hume which also concern religion or natural religion. (Try not to limit your search to too few articles.)

3. Find entries on natural religion.

4. Looking at the entries you found, what other authors have written on natural religion?

5. What other topics did Hume write on besides religion?

6. Select an interesting citation and print it. Is it available in our libraries?

16. Understanding How Databases Work by Building One in Class

Trish Ridgeway
Handley Regional Library, Winchester, Virginia

Introduction	In this exercise, students collaborate with the instruction librarian in designing a database. Students will gain a deeper understanding of database components and in turn will be more confident in their abilities to use databases.
Subject	Any
Level of Activity	Basic
Time Required	30–60 minutes (Can be completed in 30 minutes if the presenter pushes participants to move briskly.)
Size of Class	10–40
Preparation	1. Locate a one-page or shorter magazine article on a topic relevant to the group. *Newsweek* and *Time* articles work well. Choose articles that have proper names and a variety of concepts. Locate a citation of this article in a database and make a transparency of it for use later in the session.

2. Photocopy the article as a handout for the class. Add instructions for an indexing exercise to the photocopy if there is room available. The instructions include:

a. Read the article and circle every word or phrase that could be used to index or describe this article.

b. In the space below, write down any additional words or phrases that should be used as index terms but are NOT in the article.

3. Prepare as handouts or overhead transparencies:

a. Database Design Checklist (Figure 16-1).

b. Worksheet to write down the first record of the database (Figure 16-2).

c. How the exercise article is indexed in a commercial database (online or CD-ROM) (Figure 16-3).

4. Prepare materials and notes to present a training program on how to search whatever databases are appropriate for the group using concepts discovered during the class.

Class Instructions

1. *Introduction*: This exercise will closely examine database design by examining the strengths, weaknesses, and differences among various databases. Assume we are about to design a new database. The article you have is the first record we'll enter. Indexing the first article will guide us in making some design decisions. Read the article, circle indexing terms, and write down additional terms.

2. *Gather all terms*: Encourage students to call out indexing terms and write them down.

3. *Design decisions*: The instructor asks the class to look at the database design checklist (Figure 16-1). Explain that creating fields allows the computer to process information more efficiently. Choose a bibliographic citation style without an abstract. Take this time to discuss briefly the various types of formats occurring in various databases, using specific examples. Explain that the labor involved in producing each type of format, the ease of article retrieval, and the size of the database are all valid points to make when discussing design.

4. *Review the list of terms the students suggested*: Tell them that most databases use only three to five entries. Have the class decide on three. Students should base their decisions on the type of audience the database is to reach, whether to include scientific and/or popular terms, whether the database should include indexed fields for geographic names or personal names, and so on. Be warned that students will be reluctant to winnow down their lists. Begin a discussion of controlled vocabulary by asking the class the ramifications of using terms we alone generated for our new database or electing to use terms from an official list of accepted subject terms (e.g., LCSH).

5. *Constructing the first record*: Have students take pieces of the article and create fields and abbreviations for each field. Explain the advantages of compartmentalizing information in the citation to fields. Distribute or display the record for the article you are using from a real database (Figure 16-3). Even if the indexing for the article is perfect, and often it is not, students begin to see why it is important to know something about the structure of the database before searching it. Discuss some of the imperfections of database indexing here.

6. *After the exercise*: Introduce terminology and concepts needed to understand the basics of searching, using the article and design decisions the group made. The final step in the presentation is to have students work together to develop search strategies for their research questions. The instructor works with students to formulate

search statements. Depending on the technology available, students may connect to a particular database to search for information, or the instructor may search for the entire class. Use a student volunteer from the class to enter the search while others suggest commands and/or words to use.

Some students who know basic searching or those that may not want to see the broader picture may say, "Just tell me how to search." Explain that the purpose of the exercise is to teach novices the basics and to teach experienced searchers something new about a database.

After the session, students will have a more realistic view of database and indexing limits and will come to the reference desk with more intelligent questions concerning databases. If a student retrieves no records for a search, he or she might have some idea why.

FIGURE 16-1

DATABASE DESIGN CHECKLIST

Fields

_____ Record is divided into fields
_____ No fields

Record Format

_____ Bibliographic citation only
_____ Bibliographic citation with indexing terms
_____ Bibliographic citation, indexing terms, and abstract
_____ Full document

Indexing

_____ No indexing
_____ Indexing terms assigned as we feel like it
_____ Indexing terms assigned from official source (LCSH, etc.)

FIGURE 16-2

CONSTRUCTING A RECORD IN OUR DATABASE

FIGURE 16-3

OUR CITATION IN TWO DATABASES

Magazine Index (Online)   [SAMPLE ARTICLE]

AN   6564772.   8809

DB   MAGS.

TI   Everything old is new again; scientists unearth China's ancient dragons.

AU   Seligmann-Jean.

SO   Newsweek (NSWKA), volume 112, issue n8, August 22, 1988, p 57(1)

PD   880822

IL   illustration; photograph

GL   Geographic Location; China. ANCC.

DE   Paleontology; Cretaceous. Ankylosauridae; research.
       Scientific-expeditions; China. China:antiquities.

Reader's Guide (on CD)

Seligmann, Jean

Everything old is new again (baby Ankylosaurs found in China)

Newsweek v 112, p57 August 22'88

il

SUBJECT COVERED:

Dinosaurs

Paleontology/China

17. The Content and Character of Print and Electronic Indexes

Kristin Ramsdell
California State University, Hayward, California

Introduction

This short, collaborative in-class exercise is intended to help students understand:
1. What periodical indexes/databases are
2. That they are not all alike
3. That they exist in print and electronic formats
4. That their characters are determined by the periodicals they index
5. That knowing something about them is useful in planning a search strategy to use time efficiently
6. That it is just as important to know what electronic index to use as it is to know what print index to use

Subject

Any

Level of Activity

Basic to intermediate

Time Required

10 minutes

Size of Class

Maximum of 25

Preparation

1. Choose several different print indexes (e.g., *Readers' Guide, Social Sciences Index, Humanities Index, Business Periodicals Index*, etc.)
2. Select a general topic that can be found in all of the indexes (e.g., drug abuse, pollution, euthanasia). Be sure to choose volumes that illustrate the difference in coverage.
3. Look up your topic examples in each index ahead of time. NOT finding an entry for a particular topic might also serve as an example of what is not covered by a particular index.

Class Instructions

Have the students cluster in small groups of three to five and pass out one print index to each group. Have them search a topic, choose two or three articles that look interesting or relevant, and be prepared to share them with the class. You may need to provide a little help to the students while they are searching, but try to avoid telling them too much. The purpose is to allow students to discover what you want them to learn and to draw their own conclusions.

Discussion When students have located citations, have each group briefly mention the article titles and the journal titles where they were found. Ask students if they can determine a particular focus or slant in the articles. (This may take a bit of guidance.) Once a conclusion is reached, ask them to announce the title of the index used to the class. At this point students should be making a connection between article title, journal title, and subject index. When the group work is finished, reinforce by asking questions like "Are all indexes alike?" "If not, how do they differ?" and "How would this help you when you are looking for information?" Conclude by mentioning that electronic databases are organized in the same way as their print counterparts and that it is just as important (maybe even more so) to select an appropriate database as it is to select an appropriate print index.

18. Searching Print and CD-ROM Indexes: A Comparison

Nena V. Thomas
Curtis Laws Wilson Library, University of Missouri, Rolla, Missouri

Introduction

This cooperative learning exercise, designed for use in an electronic classroom, is meant to be adaptable for a variety of subjects. Time spent on this exercise may be adjusted by eliminating an index, not printing in class, or requiring completion of the exercise outside of class time. Before students begin hands-on work, a librarian or teacher should demonstrate and explain basic electronic search concepts. Time is allotted for in-class evaluations.

Subject

Any

Level of Activity

Basic

Time Required

50–60 minutes

Size of Class

20

Preparation

1. Produce transparencies of appropriate print index pages.
2. Photocopy "Searching Print and CD-ROM Indexes" exercise sheets (Figure 18-1) and distribute to students.
3. Instructor must have in-class access to CD-ROMs and online catalog.

Class Instructions

1. Divide into groups (five students per group).
2. Give each group one exercise sheet. (Half of the groups receive exercises for print indexes, and the other half for CD-ROM indexes.)
3. After the exercise is completed, switch places so that "print groups" work on CD-ROMS and vice versa.
4. Discuss what the students found and which print indexes and databases they think are best for the sample topics. How did they decide?
5. Demonstrate the online catalog and how to find the periodicals cited by the indexes.

Discussion   Results assessment is not incorporated into this exercise. At minimum, librarians using this exercise are encouraged to have students discuss findings before the demonstration of the online catalog. Ideally, librarians should collect the exercises and examine individual results.

FIGURE 18-1
SEARCHING PRINT AND CD-ROM INDEXES

The purpose of this exercise is to discover how to use both print and CD-ROM indexes to find articles in journals. Once you find the articles on your subject, you would need to use the online catalog to see if the library owns the journal and to find the call number and location of the journal. The librarian will demonstrate this step. Remember: The library does not own all of the periodicals included in these indexes.

PRINT INDEXES

1. How is the *Readers' Guide* arranged? Choose any or all of the following:
Author_____
Title_____
Subject_____
(**Hint**: See "Prefatory Notes" on pages in the front of the index.)

2. Is the *Social Sciences Index* arranged in the same manner?

3. Some of the journal titles are abbreviated. How would you find the full title of the journal? (**Hint**: Indexes usually have an explanation of how to use them on the pages in the front.)

4. Look for articles under the subject heading "Gun Control" in the *Social Sciences Index*. Are there any articles? What other subject headings are suggested? You will see that there are subheadings for this subject (in bold print).

5. Look for articles under the subject heading "Gun Control" in *Readers' Guide*. Are there any articles? Are the articles the same ones that you found in the *Social Sciences Index*?

6. Try the same search in *The New York Times Index*. Are there any articles under the subject "Gun Control"? Are you given another subject? Remember: If the index does not have your subject heading, it does not necessarily mean that there are no articles. Each index has its own indexing system.

7. What other subject headings did you find?

8. Choose an article that might be interesting for a research paper on the subject "Gun Control." Use either the *Social Sciences Index* or the *Readers' Guide*. Write down all of the information that you will need to find the article (author and title of the article; title, issue, and number of the journal; and page numbers). We will try to find the article when we have finished learning about indexes.

FIGURE 18-1 cont.

9. Try the subject "Hispanics" in all three of the indexes (*The New York Times Index*, *Humanities Index*, and the *Social Sciences Index*). Note that the subject headings in each index are not necessarily the same. Write the different headings to look for when you are searching the subject "Hispanics."

CD-ROM INDEXES

CD-ROM indexes, like their counterpart print indexes, are subject specific. Be sure that you understand the coverage of CD-ROM indexes, or you may not find anything on your subject. (Example: *Compendex* is an engineering index and would not be a good choice to search the subject "Endangered Species".)

ProQuest GPO is a CD-ROM index containing citations to general-interest periodicals and newspapers in print, on microfilm, or on CD-ROM. *(The library may not own all of the periodicals indexed.)*

1. Select "Search using multiple keywords" (Boolean).

2. Type "Gun Control." How many articles are there? Can you narrow the search?

3. One way to narrow the search is to look at the first few articles. When you find one that might be interesting, look at the subject headings listed in the abstract. Use one of the subject headings to narrow your search.

4. Type **#1 and** the subject you have selected. (You must type the word "and" in between each word unless you want the two words to be adjacent to each other in the title or abstract.)

5. If you still found too many, try to narrow your search by searching "gun control" and "violent crime."

6. Perhaps you would like to find *more* articles. Erase "violent crime" and type "crime?" Did this give you more articles? (The question mark will search for all words that begin with the letters preceding the question mark.)

7. Try the index first (F6). Search for subject. Search for the word "Hispanics." Is this listed as a subject? What is the subject?

8. Using the keyword index, search for "Acculturation." (Notice the two words are searched together.) How many articles did you find?

FIGURE 18-1 cont.

9. Now, find an article under this search that was published in *The Hispanic Journal of Behavioral Sciences* entitled "Substance Use Among Texas Hispanics and Non-Hispanics." Is the article on a CD? If it is, press the Enter key to see the abstract and the Enter key again to see which CD it is on.

10. Select the CD and put it into the image drive. If you have trouble reading the article, press F8 (enlarge). F7 will reduce the size.

11. The number of pages are listed at the top of your screen (PgDn key will put you on the next page and PgUp key will give you the previous page.) Read the top of your screen for printing information.

19. "Berry Picking": Pre-focus Exploration of Student Research Topics

Mary Jane Petrowski
Colgate University, Hamilton, New York

Introduction	1. Introduce research as a *process*.
	2. The student understands that an initial question may be too broad or too narrow to investigate effectively. Adjustment in scope, direction, or time frame may be needed.
	3. The student understands the importance of pre-focus exploration and strategies for undertaking focus formulation.
	4. The student recognizes that information needed to identify information sources is manipulated into systematic sequences called "citations" and that the amount of information required and citation form may vary from field to field.
	5. The student understands that no access tool is comprehensive in scope.
	6. The student understands how to identify the source field in a periodical citation and to use that information to determine local holdings for that source using the online catalog or holdings list.
	7. The student recognizes that periodicals may be grouped together by title or call number in order to provide ease of use.
	8. The student understands that their "home library" is not the only location containing periodicals.
	9. The student recognizes that libraries do not have comprehensive holdings and that one library may lend an item from its collection or furnish a copy of an item from its collection to another library not under the same administration.
Subject	Any
Level of Activity	Basic
Time Required	in class: 20–30 minutes
Size of Class	10–20
Preparation	1. Develop and produce transparencies based on Figures 19-1 and 19-2.
	2. Copy handouts based on Figure 19-1.

3. Develop or make available prepared handouts that list periodical databases, reference sources, and other services the class will use.

Class Instructions

1. Students are asked to form groups of two or three, depending on the number of available workstations in the reference area or electronic classroom.

2. Distribute copies of the Model of the Research Process (Kuhlthau, 1988) (Figure 19-1) to all students and present a brief lecture and demonstration as outlined here:

    A. Find a Pattern. Show the "Find a Pattern" (Von Oech, 1989) overhead transparency (Figure 19-2). Much of what is called "intelligence" is our ability to recognize patterns. We recognize sequences (DNA structure), cycles (bird migration, the seasons), processes (how to convert grape juice to wine), tendencies, fads, shapes, and probabilities.

    B. Research as a Process. Premise: Students do not understand research as a process, particularly as a creative process involving time for reflection and gestation. An overhead transparency of the Kulhthau model of the information search process is introduced (Figure 19-1). The creative but difficult stages of pre-focus exploration and focus formulation are highlighted along with strategies for working through those stages.

    C. Review Research Strategies for Pre-focus Exploration. Refer to handouts where particular reference resources, article databases, and Web resources are listed. Emphasize that "berry picking" or "trolling the databases" are extremely important initial activities in the exploration process.

    D. Online Demo: Way into the Databases. At this point a quick online demo is given. Students are instructed to circle the various menu choices that will lead them to a particular database (if OPAC menu structures are confusing)

3. Each person takes turns looking up his/her topic in one of the recommended databases. Each student has a handout with directions for connecting to the various databases. Students are encouraged to help each other while the librarian and faculty member circulate as coaches and troubleshooters.

4. Each student finds one reference that looks interesting or relevant and prints out the citation.

5. The student must then determine whether the university library owns the source cited in the reference.

6. If the library owns the source (usually a journal), the student retrieves it. If the library does not own the title, the student fills out an interlibrary loan form.
7. All work is handed in during the session for quick review and feedback.

Evaluation

First-year students and teaching faculty find this kind of session very useful for a variety of reasons. Both students and faculty (in many cases) are using databases for the very first time. More experienced students—always a few—are pleased to help novice searchers. Students leave the session feeling they have learned something and that information on their topic exists. They learn how to read a citation, locate the title of a periodical, and figure out whether the library owns it. They experience finding a journal title on the shelf. The students appreciate learning basic skills instead of having someone lecture through this information. "Free" interlibrary loan service is inevitably new information. Faculty unaccustomed to using databases have an opportunity to learn along with students.

REFERENCES
Kuhlthau, C. C. (1988). Developing a model of the library search process: cognitive and affective aspects. *RQ* 28, 232–42.
Von Oech, R. (1989). *Creative Whack Pack*. Stamford, Conn.: U. S. Games Systems.

FIGURE 19-1
Kuhlthau Model of the Search Process

STAGES	Task Initiation	Topic Selection	Pre-focus Exploration	Focus Formulation	Information Collection	Search Closure	Starting Writing
feelings	uncertainty	optimism	confusion/ frustration/ doubt	clarity	Sense of direction/ confidence	relief	satisfaction or dissatisfaction
thoughts	ambiguity		specificity				
			increased interest				
actions	seeking relevant information				seeking pertinent information		

Kuhlthau, C. C. (1988). Developing a model of the library search process: Cognitive and affective aspects. *RQ* 28, 232–42.

FIGURE 19–2

FIND A PATTERN

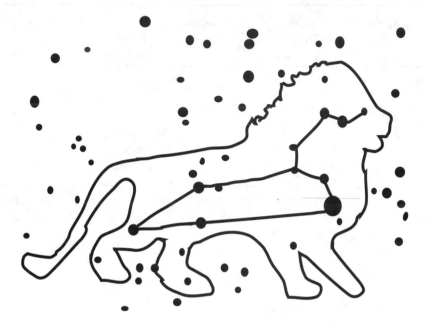

Much of what is called "intelligence" is our ability to recognize patterns. We recognize sequences (the order in which you put on your clothes), cycles (bird migrations), processes (how to convert flour, eggs, and milk into waffles), tendencies (if I smile at the checkout-counter girl, she'll smile at me), shapes (the stars that make up the constellation Leo), and probablilities (the likelihood of throwing a "seven" at a crap table). **What patterns can you use to better understand your idea?**

Von Oech, R. (1989) *Creative Whack Pack*. Stanford: U.S. Games Systems.

20. Involving Group Teams in Selecting Appropriate Indexes and Keywords

Kimberley Donnelly and Brian Sacolic
Farley Library, Wilkes University, Wilkes-Barre, Pennsylvania

Introduction	Students are assigned to develop a proposal for a group project. Working together, students learn the differences between subject and general periodical databases, understand which databases are more appropriate for their topics, and construct successful keyword searches.
Subject	Any
Level of Activity	Basic, although the session requires a high level of group participation.
Time Required	50 minutes
Size of Class	Maximum of 30, with six groups of four to five students each

Preparation

1. Prepare the following handouts and transparencies:
   a. A list of computerized indexes in your library with annotations indicating coverage (Figure 20-1)
   b. Worksheets for groups to fill out and hand in to instructor (Figure 20-2) (The worksheet should include spaces for keywords and selected databases to be listed. You may also include a section to be completed after class requiring students to locate and record citations for useful items.)
   c. Handouts for searching individual databases (optional)
   d. Transparencies with definitions of "keyword" and "subject heading"
2. You will need access to the library's electronic classroom or computerized databases and the ability to project search screens to the audience.
3. Prepare sample topics that are appropriate for the databases to be demonstrated.

Class Instructions

1. Ask students to sit with their group members as they enter the classroom. **[2 minutes]**
2. Welcome students, and outline the purpose of the session. **[2 minutes]**

3. Explain the purpose and nature of proposal writing. Looking at others' published research can give ideas on how to proceed. Once they have determined a successful solution to a problem or question from extant research, it can be adapted for their own needs. **[2 minutes]**

4. Ask students to have a group project topic ready, and distribute the worksheet. Have each group elect a participant for the live demo and another as group recorder, who will be responsible for completing and turning in the worksheet. **[3 minutes]**

5. Explain that all library databases operate in similar ways but that different commands and keystrokes are used for each one. Define "subject headings/descriptors" and "keywords" using the transparency. **[3 minutes]**

6. Tell the groups to take three to four minutes to come up with a list of relevant keywords to be recorded on the worksheet. Include as many synonyms and phrases as possible. Circulate among the groups, and encourage as needed. **[5 minutes]**

7. Discuss library databases. Stress that some index books and others index (and abstract) journal articles. Explain the difference between general and subject-specific databases. Stress the importance of selecting the appropriate databases for the project. Distribute the list of in-house library databases (online, CD-ROM, etc.). **[3 minutes]**

8. Have groups choose appropriate indexes from the list and write them on the worksheet. Circulate and assist where needed. Make a list of each group, their topic, and which index they want to use. **[6 minutes]**

9. Begin searching the databases. With the list of topics and databases, start with the simplest databases and lead to the complex. Have each group's demo participant bring the worksheet and come forward to operate the keyboard. Ease the anxiety of the participant by indicating that the librarian will assist. Have the leader state the group's topic and the database chosen. Demonstrate how the database is accessed. Have the participant read the keywords to the class. Walk the participant through the process. **[18 minutes]**

10. Explain parts of a citation. When a keyword search pulls up a useful item, show the class the subject headings/descriptors. Demonstrate how to use these terms to find more useful items. **[2 minutes]**

11. Explain how to locate journals in the library. **[2 minutes]**

12. Address questions, concerns, or comments from students in the remaining time.

Discussion

This first-year workshop may be the first encounter students have with the library. Guiding the student's choice of keywords helps them succeed. Avoiding a long lecture through active participation in an encouraging atmosphere will maintain interest and increase retention.

When demonstrating databases, attempt to show the similarities and downplay the differences. Show that databases are essentially alike, but the information is arranged differently, and the subjects that are covered vary.

Students with computer skills are an asset, so use them. Many students are more interested in what a peer does at the workstation than what a librarian might do. Student interest in this session is maintained because they are starting to work on a project and they may be called in front to do the next demonstration.

FIGURE 20-1

COMPUTERIZED INDEXES TO PERIODICALS

All of the databases listed below are available in the library for public use. You may search for articles and print the citations (and abstracts when available) for free. This list is intended to give you a brief overview of the topics covered by each database.

Broad coverage databases:
1. *EXPANDED ACADEMIC INDEX* (InfoTrac): Nearly all subjects and topics are covered, especially current events. Includes indexing to the last six months of the *New York Times*.
2. *HUMANITIES INDEX*: Covers archaeology, classical studies, communication, folklore, history, language, literature, performing arts (music, dance, theater), philosophy, religion, and related subjects.
3. *SOCIAL SCIENCES INDEX*: Anthropology, community health and medical care, economics, geography, gerontology, international relations, law and criminology, social work and public welfare, sociology, and related subjects.
4. *GENERAL SCIENCES INDEX*: Astronomy, atmospheric science, biology, botany, chemistry, computers, earth sciences, environment, food and nutrition, genetics, mathematics, medicine and health, microbiology, physics, physiology, and zoology.

Specialized coverage databases:
5. *APPLIED SCIENCE AND TECHNOLOGY INDEX*: Aeronautics and space science, chemistry, computer technology and applications, construction industry, energy, engineering, environment, geology, machinery, mathematics, mineralogy, oceanography, petroleum and gas, plastics, transportation, and other industrial and mechanical arts topics.
6. *BUSINESS PERIODICALS INDEX*: Accounting, advertising and marketing, banking, communications, computer technology and applications, economics, finance and investments, insurance, international business, management and personnel administration, pharmaceuticals, public relations, public utilities, real estate, transportation, and related topics.
7. *BIOLOGICAL AND AGRICULTURAL INDEX*: Agriculture and agricultural economics, biochemistry, botany, ecology, food science, forestry, genetics, horticulture, marine biology, nutrition, soil science, environmental science, veterinary medicine, and zoology.
8. *MEDLINE*: All areas of medical science.
9. *HEALTHPLAN*: Non-clinical aspects of health care delivery (i.e., health administration).
10. *CINAHL (CUMULATIVE INDEX TO NURSING AND ALLIED HEALTH)*: Comprehensive database of citations to nursing and allied health literature.
11. *ERIC (EDUCATIONAL RESOURCES INFORMATION CENTER)*: All topics relating to education.
12. *ENVIRONMENT ABSTRACTS*: All topics relating to the environment: population, recycling, waste management, research.

FIGURE 20-2

TECHNOLOGICAL SURVIVAL LIBRARY WORK FORM

Recorder _____

Demonstration participant _____

Members _____

Group topic _____

Instructor and class time _____

ACTIVITY 1: Developing a list of key words and phrases. Break your group topic into its main concepts and make a list of key terms for each concept.
An example is in brackets.

Concept 1	Concept 2	Concept 3
[urban]	[revitalization]	

ACTIVITY 2: Selecting databases. Use the list of Computerized Indexes to Periodicals to determine appropriate database(s) to search. List selected databases below:

ACTIVITY 3: Locating citations. For the next class period, locate and print the bibliographic citations for three relevant articles. Turn in the printouts and this completed work form at the next class meeting.

21. Constructing Research Statements and Brainstorming for Keywords

Stacey Nickell
Paducah Community College, Paducah, Kentucky

Introduction	The objective of this exercise is to encourage creative thinking in the research process. After developing and analyzing a research statement in class, students are given an opportunity to brainstorm for synonyms in a collaborative environment.
Subject	Any
Level of Activity	Basic
Time Required	Preparation time: Transparencies, 60 minutes (one time only); Class time, 50 minutes
Size of Class	25–30 students
Preparation	1. Prepare lecture transparency (Figure 21-1).
	2. Prepare in-class worksheet (Figure 21-2) and group transparencies (Figure 21-3).
	3. Prepare sample research statements.
Class Instructions	1. Review critical thinking skills needed for conducting research in an electronic environment, including Boolean logic, truncating, and nesting. Begin the lecture by explaining how to construct search statements. Illustrate examples of broad and narrow statements. Use the sample research statement "What are the effects of television violence on children?" as an example, and take students through the process.
	2. Divide the class into groups of two to four students. Give each group a sample research statement and in-class worksheet. Show the transparency with the instructions to identify main ideas and provide synonyms for each idea. Students then select the main ideas/concepts and brainstorm for synonyms. Remind students to try a variety of keywords as well as subject searches. Each group searches two databases or indexes to locate information on their topic and compares results. Students return to class and report results to the entire class.

Discussion   During the discussion, students can be told about the features of the databases used in the exercise. Use this time to explain the scope (subject–specific vs. general) and audience (academic vs. mainstream) of the database. Sample research statements may include the following:

1. What is the relationship between educational level and salary?
2. Is AIDS among women in the United States steadily increasing?
3. Is there a relationship between crime and poverty?
4. What effect do computers have on the way business is conducted?
5. Does legalized gambling subsidize organized crime?

FIGURE 21-1
Sample Topic Transparency

TOPIC: What are the effects of television violence on children?

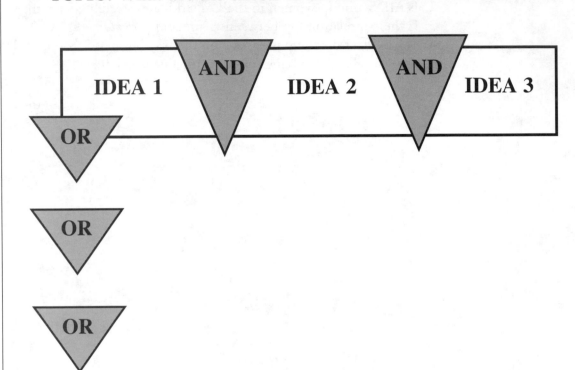

FIGURE 21–2

ENGLISH COMPOSITION 101 CLASS WORKSHEET

<u>**GROUP ASSIGNMENT**</u>: Brainstorm assigned topics, identify, synonyms for each concept, and list them in the appropriate columns. Complete the diagram on the attached transparency film as shown below. Construct search strategies for use on the computer systems by connecting words within the columns with the **OR** operator. Connect words or groups of words from other columns with the **AND** operator.

This assignment does not have "cut and dry," right and wrong answers. You are trying to develop different kinds of search strategies to locate information on the library computers.

EXAMPLE: How do antibiotics affect bacterial infections:

IDEA 1 — AND	IDEA 2 — AND	IDEA 3
antibiotic?	Affect	Infection?
Drug?	Effect	Bacteria?
Medicin?	Impact	Septic?
Therapy	Influence	Disease?
Remedy	Work	
Cure	Fight	

(The left column words are connected with **OR** operators.)

K= (antibiotic? **or** drug? **or** medicin?) and (infection? **or** disease?)

K= antibiotic? **and** (infection? or bacteria? **or** septic? **or** disease?)

K= antibiotic.su **and** (affect **or** influence) **and** (disease **or** bacteria?)

NOTE: Write on the attached transparency film <u>ONLY</u> with the supplied marker.

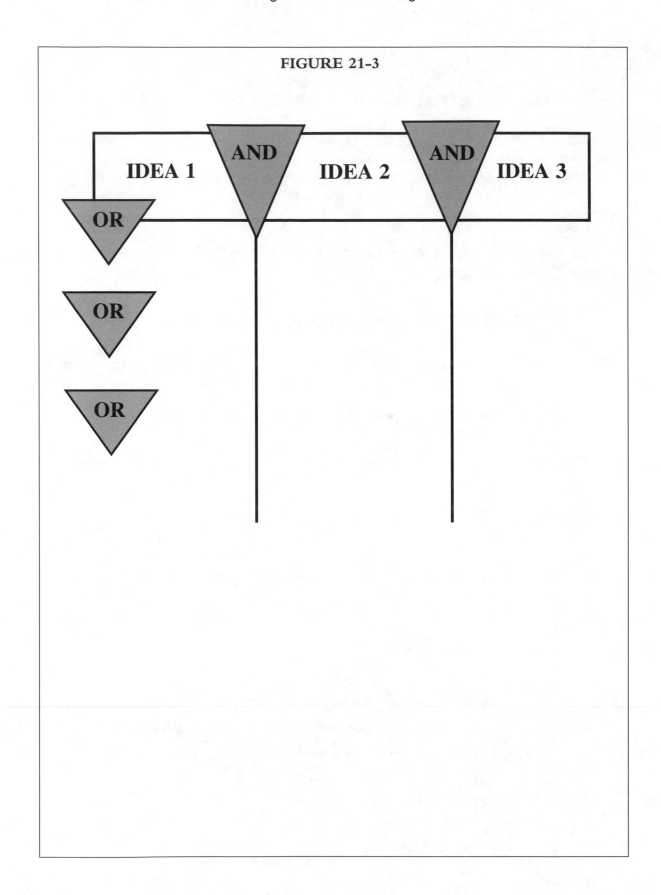

FIGURE 21-3

22. Human versus Machine ("Free Text") Indexing

Christopher J. Hoeppner
DePaul University Libraries, Chicago, Illinois

Introduction

Students use indexes, but they probably don't understand the processes by which they are created. This exercise introduces the concepts of human-generated versus computer-generated indexing by comparing and contrasting the effectiveness of each.

Subject

Any

Level of Activity

Basic

Time Required

Preparation time (one time only): 2–3 hours to identify an appropriate article and prepare handouts and transparencies. In-class time: 10–15 minutes.

Size of Class

Maximum of forty, in groups of four to six

Preparation

1. Select an article from a publication indexed in four to six differently focused indexes (e.g., general news, education, business, computing, social sciences, health). Make sufficient copies of the article for all students. If the article is long, copy only the first and last pages. One article I have used: Konrad, Walecia. "I'd toddle a mile for a Camel." *Business Week*, December 23, 1991, p. 34.
2. In the classroom, prepare two crude drawings on a blackboard or flip chart. Make one drawing of two human stick figures with a double-ended arrow between the two and the other of a computer and a human stick figure with a double-ended arrow between them.
3. Write the various subject areas of the article on the board or flip chart. (A variation of this exercise asks students to identify possible subject areas. See "class instructions" below for details.)
4. Organize students into task groups. In the interest of time, do so with a minimum of movement.

Class Instructions

1. Point to the drawings. Inform the class that you will explain the importance of machine vs. human indexing and how it can affect the outcome of a search in the library. Begin by explaining that indexing:

   a. is the process of arranging information in a way that it can be readily found;

   b. is created by people or machines, with noticeably different results;

   c. varies based on the index's intended audience (e.g., physicians, scholars, general public).

2. For the next two minutes, have the class read as much of the article as they can. Pose the question: "If it were your job to index this article for a particular audience of researchers, what words or short phrases would you use to capture the essence of the article's content?"

[VARIATION ONE – After two minutes' reading time, ask: "What types of readers or researchers might be interested in the subject matter of this article?" Have students discuss this for about 30 seconds, then write down several (enough for the number of groups) of the subject areas/audience they suggest on the board.]

Assign a subject focus and a particular audience to each student group. Ask them to assign several words or short phrases to represent the article's content with the audience in mind. Have each group elect an individual to record terms on the board. Allow the groups three to five minutes to work. Proceed with discussion below.

(Optional: In a session with a broader focus, this step could lead into a discussion of library organization, LC or Dewey classification.)

Discussion

After students have written terms on the board, remark on the similarity and difference in terms. Point out that more specific terms are likely to be used in a particular subject index than in a general one, so students should keep this in mind when using indexes.

Contrast this with computer-generated indexing, which uses the brute power of the computer to create an index of every nontrivial word in a record (including those in the citation and abstract). One can then search by keyword. Most electronic databases offer this kind of indexing, also known as keyword or "free-text" searching. Some, but not all, also use human filtering to make content judgments and to assign appropriate terms. Computer-generated indexing yields different results for two reasons:

1. Terms assigned by human indexers might not be *literally* represented in document text but are relevant, preventing the document from being retrieved from a computer-generated index.

2. Terms in a document might not *precisely* reflect document content, leading to the retrieval of irrelevant documents. (Point out examples of how each of these differences could arise with the article from the exercise.) In the cigarette article cited above, the following conclusions could be drawn:

   • A business manager seeking articles about "cigarette advertising" or "marketing" might be interested in this article.

   • Human indexers might assign such terms to the article, but a free-text searching using either of these would not find it.

   • The article would be found with a free-text search on "alcohol advertising," even though this is not really the article's focus.

Acknowledge that human indexing requires judgment and is not perfect. Computer-generated indexing is not necessarily inferior to human indexing. Researchers should use both types of indexing when available.

Demonstrate a library database using controlled vocabulary, subject headings, or descriptors. To contrast, search the database by keyword. If time allows, explore a database and limit the search to keyword only.

The Yahoo service (http://www.yahoo.com) can provide comparison and contrast to the discussion. Yahoo is indexed manually but can be searched as free text also. Using a prepared example or one from a student in the class, contrast the results of a free-text search for certain keywords with the results retrieved using the manual indexing for a designated subset of the Yahoo database. Look at the number of items retrieved by each search and scan each list for items that appear to be unique to one search or the other.

23. Staying Current in Your Field Using Indexes

Carol J. Scamman
Steen Library, Stephen F. Austin State University, Nacogdoches, Texas

Introduction	This exercise was developed for use in an electronic classroom. The exercise will demonstrate and suggest ways to stay current within a discipline. Students will also understand how search terms can be combined to yield better results.
Subject	Any
Level of Activity	Basic
Time Required	1.25 to 1.5 hours (It can be adapted for shorter class periods.)
Size of Class	Approximately 20
Preparation	1. Consult with teaching faculty about assigning groups and topics before the library session.
	2. Give the faculty member the handout "Hints for Successful Active Learning Exercises" (Figure 23-1).
	3. Give each group an exercise sheet (Figure 23-2) and a copy of "Key Concepts and Terminology" (Figure 23-3).
	4. Write group members' names and topics on exercise sheets.
	5. Prepare materials (transparencies, etc.) for demonstration of search terms and techniques.
Class Instructions	1. Explain to the class that the purpose of the exercise is:
	a. to discover resources that can be used across the curriculum;
	b. to explore ways of staying current in their field;
	c. to understand how search terms can be combined;
	d. to develop critical thinking skills about search results.
	2. Each group appoints a recorder to write down what the group did on the exercise sheets and a reporter who will fill in the class on the results. Have each student in the group record his or her name on the sheet.
	3. Remind students that the exercise is a group effort and that the librarian and professor are present only as facilitators.

4. Encourage those who have the least amount of experience to do the actual searching; students with more experience can act as "coaches."

5. Reserve the last 15–20 minutes for group reports and discussion.

Discussion

Evaluation sheets are an important component of this exercise. Have students complete them before leaving the library. An alternative would be to provide evaluation sheets to the professor to be returned to the librarian as soon as possible.

FIGURE 23-1

Hints for Successful Active Learning Exercises

Before the library session:

1. Assign students to groups (or have them choose their own).

2. Have the students choose a reporter and a recorder. It's preferable for the recorder to be someone who already has searched electronic indexes, so that the less experienced users will get more hands-on practice.

3. Assign or let the students choose the topics they will research. This will allow them to benefit from the instruction and from what they find in class.

4. Provide the librarian with a printed list of the topics and the groups assigned to them.

During the library session:

1. Hand out one learning exercise per group. This will encourage them to work together and let them know what is expected of them.

2. Emphasize that the students will be learning from and teaching each other and that they will get as much out of the session as they put into it. Explain your role as a facilitator and that you expect to learn from them, too.

3. In class, encourage the less experienced users to take turns searching. Let the more experienced users "coach" them.

4. During the class, let the students know five to ten minutes before they are to stop or change an activity.

5. Allow approximately fifteen minutes for the groups to report and another five to summarize and comment on their findings.

FIGURE 23-2

ELECTRONIC SEARCH STRATEGIES

Faculty Name_____Date_____

Course Number, Title_____

You will be asked to work in groups. The purpose of this exercise is to learn about electronic library resources that can assist you in the following ways:
- To discover resources that can be used across the curriculum
- To explore ways of staying current in your field
- To understand how search terms can be combined
- To develop critical thinking skills about search results

NAMES OF GROUP MEMBERS:

TOPIC:

PROCEDURE:

1. Choose a recorder to write down the search terms you use and how you combine them.

2. Choose a reporter who will explain to the class what you have discovered.

3. The reporter will need to answer the following questions:

a. What search terms did your groups use and how were they combined and entered? Use the blackboard or overhead projector.

    Index A:

    Index B:

FIGURE 23-2 cont.

b. How many references did you get on your topic?

Index A:

Index B:

c. Describe the reference that your group thought was most relevant, and explain why your group thinks it's the best one.

d. What kinds of problems did your group have with the search? What things went well?

4. The teacher and librarian will be facilitators for this exercise and wrap up the session after the reporters have given the group reports.

QUESTIONS

A. Use the **Expanded Academic Index** (InfoTrac) or the **General Business File** (InfoTrac) to find an article on your topic. Print the reference to the article. Include a copy of the abstract if one is available.

B. From the Program Manager Screen, choose an icon, and find the title of another index that would be useful for your topic.

C. If time permits, search the index you named in section B (above) or search one of the FirstSearch databases. Print one reference in class if there is time.

FIGURE 23-3

KEY CONCEPTS AND TERMINOLOGY

AND, OR, NOT	Connecting words (Boolean operators) for combining terms in a search
* ? +	Common symbols for truncating (chopping off) words to search singulars and plurals and variant endings. ***** and **?** are the most commonly used. Example: **female*** finds both female and females in many, but not all, of our electronic indexes.
RECORD	The description of a document (article, book, etc.) found in a search.
FIELDS	The various parts of a record, such as author, title, abstract, publication year. These are usually searchable separately.
FIELD LABELS	Symbols that are used to indicate various parts of a record. Common symbols include JN for journal, PT for publication type, PY or PD for publication year or publication date. Also known as "tags."
LIMITS	Field labels that can be used in a search to limit results by something such as publication year, publication type, or language. Examples: **la=english** or **english in la**
DESCRIPTORS	The subject indexing terms used to describe the contents of a document. Common field labels for descriptors are DE or SU. Used to obtain more precise search results. There is often a built-in thesaurus of descriptors from which you can insert terms into your search strategy.
NESTING	Enclosing search terms within parentheses with the word OR between words. This allows the searching of several words as a group. Examples: **(shakespeare or marlowe) and staging** **(gun or firearms) and control and (law* or legislation)**

24. Searching Indexes to Challenge "Expert" Information

Karen Paul Topham
Brookdale Community College, Lincroft, New Jersey

Introduction

Exercises coupled with a topic search are more successful than "canned searches" prepared in advance by a librarian. Using a controversial article from the op-ed pages of local or national newspapers, students read the article in class and determine whether additional information is needed. Students formulate search statements, select appropriate databases containing needed information, and evaluate the accuracy of what they find. This approach is useful when the content professor wants to introduce students to electronic searching but has no particular research topic on which to concentrate. This type of activity can be done in one session using only electronic periodical indexes. It can be adapted to sessions with other databases, print sources, government documents, etc.

Five Minute Cogitation (Optional)
• At the beginning of the session, ask "What do you hope to add to your understanding of the research process after this session?"
• At the end of the session, ask: "What new clue or skill have you developed during this session that you can share with your fellow students, friends, etc.?"

Subject

Any

Level of Activity

Basic to intermediate

Time Required

45 minutes

Size of Class

No limit

Preparation

Find an attention-grabbing "viscerally challenging" article. One example is from the "In America" column by Bob Herbert, *New York Times*, July 3, 1995, page 21. The article, "Let Them Eat Poison," begins with the death of a young boy who had eaten a hamburger tainted by *E. coli*.

Class Instructions

1. Have the students read the article quickly and write down any questions that come to mind. Instruct them to question the author's facts, arguments and position. For the above example, questions have been asked about *E. coli*, salmonella, meat processing, restaurant food handling, Department of Agriculture standards and "unscrupulous Republicans." **[5 minutes]**

2. As a group, decide on databases to search, and then develop a search strategy. A beginning question might be "What is *E. coli*?" **[17 minutes]**

3. Students break up into groups of three and four each to search different threads of the article. Different indexes, such as *Business Index, Expanded Academic Index, Health Index*, or *CINAHL* can be used. The "subgroups" try to find as much information as possible about their thread. **[15 minutes]**

Discussion

Reconvene the class, and discuss whether the findings support or contradict the author's argument. Decide whether more information is warranted, and continue searching if needed.

25. Teaching Boolean Operators in a Flash Using a Deck of Cards

Loanne Snavely
Pennsylvania State University, University Park, Pennsylvania

Introduction	Boolean operators are important tools in online searching. In this exercise, playing cards are used to illustrate how they work. Boolean operators are better understood through an active learning exercise in which all students participate, simplifying the idea of variables in a set to something all students are familiar with. An optional follow-up exercise using citations instead of cards can be used as reinforcement. This is a good exercise for those who have not introduced active learning before and want to start "small" because it can be done quickly in a primarily lecture class or added to other active learning exercises.
Subject	Any
Level of Activity	Basic
Time Required	No preparation time for the basic activity. If using the optional exercise (first time only), less than an hour is needed to prepare the exercise. Actual in-class activity time is 5 minutes (add another 10 minutes for the optional exercise).
Size of Class	Any
Preparation	1. Secure one or more decks of regular playing cards so that each student has one card. If there are fewer than 52 students in the class, it is helpful to sort the deck before the exercise. The concepts will be shown more clearly if you know which categories are represented. For example, remove all cards with a face value of less than 8. 2. [OPTIONAL EXERCISE] Prepare an exercise sheet on a topic relevant to the subject of the class. This should include a printout from a subject database listing 10–12 citations. The citations should be selected from the search statement x AND (y OR z). y and z should be synonyms. Some citations should have only y or z, while other citations should have both. To streamline the exercise, the terms in question should be underlined or highlighted.

3. Distribute one exercise sheet to each student.
4. Place one card on each student's seat before the class begins. (If this isn't possible, cards can be passed out before the exercise.)

Class Instructions   Begin by telling the class that Boolean operators are commands used to extract information from a database by combining terms in a particular way. Boolean operators consist of "AND" and "OR" ("NOT" is rarely useful, but it can be mentioned here). Explain that the terms have very specific meanings and do not necessarily mean the same as they do in everyday language (e.g., if a waitress is asking if you want orange, grapefruit or tomato juice with your breakfast, she does not mean you can have all three). "AND" means all terms must be part of the set and "OR" means any one term can be a part of the set. Have the students look at their playing cards and come up with a list of characteristics that describe the card (colors/suits/number/face). The exercise can be done with one or more suits. Some students have never played cards and don't know spades from clubs, so it might be better to use color, face, and number.

Run the following searches. Ask students holding a card that meets the criteria to raise their hands or stand up. Have students look around the room to view the search results.

1. (face card AND red card)
2. (face card OR red card) These first two searches really show the broadening versus narrowing power of these two operators.
3. Ask for several other combinations, including very broad ones (black or red) and very narrow ones (black and queen).
4. Ask for more complex combinations ((face OR ace) and red). Write this one on the board and explain nesting.

Each search you perform forces the student to think about the characteristics of his or her card and whether it fits the search criteria. The show of hands illustrates the broadening and narrowing function.

Continue the discussion by moving from the card characteristics to words in a database. If you are using the optional exercise, show how keywords selected from a citation that are combined would cause them to either be retrieved in a search or not picked up at all. Ask students to review the citations and put a checkmark by all of the citations that would be retrieved using the search "xxx and yyy," and an 'x' by all of the citations "yyy OR zzz". Allow no more than 5 minutes, or until most of the class has finished. Ask for questions and comments. As a final question, ask students which citations would have been retrieved with x AND (y OR z). Call attention to the fact that using only one of the synonyms y or z would have caused some valuable citations to be missed.

26. Human Boolean Exercise

Paula R. Dempsey   *Beth Mark*
DePaul University Library   *Messiah College Library*
Chicago, Illinois   *Grantham, Pennsylvania*

Introduction	This exercise introduces students to library databases by explaining database purpose and structure (e.g., records and fields) using common everyday examples. The importance of Boolean operators is reinforced by class participation in a physical demonstration.
Subject	Any
Level of Activity	Basic
Time Required	Preparation: 20 minutes; in-class, 15 minutes
Size of Class	15–30
Preparation	1. The librarian prepares a form that will ask students the following information: Full name, sex, year in school, home area code, date of birth (month/day), color of the shirt or blouse student is wearing today (white, other solid color, pattern) and corrected vision (no correction, glasses, contact lenses).
	2. The form is distributed to students at the beginning of the session with instructions to complete it. Form is collected and used later in the session.
Class Instructions	1. The librarian begins by introducing the concept of databases using everyday examples, such as hospital records, motor vehicle records, university student records, etc. Examples of library-related databases are given, discussing similarities and differences between book and periodical databases and the difference between general and specialized periodical indexes. Librarian emphasizes the underlying concept of all databases: organization, storage and retrieval of information.
	2. Librarian reminds students of the data collected on each of the forms. Each member of the class is now a record, comprised of several fields. Information about the class can be retrieved by search-

ing these fields. Using Boolean operators AND and OR, and truncation, the librarian creates search examples using the class:
1. DOB (April OR May OR Ju?) and AREA CODE(312)
2. YEAR (freshman OR sophomore) and SHIRT(pattern)

Physical activity has been proven to stimulate brain activity. Movement during this exercise provides an educational illustration of the information to be learned. The librarian reads a search to the class and asks class members to stand if they meet the search parameters. To illustrate the narrowing aspect of AND, add an additional search parameter to the students standing and have them sit if they meet it. Follow this exercise with a live demonstration from a library database.

OPTIONAL EXERCISE DELIVERY
Begin with a broad category (e.g., all students/faculty who have library cards) and have students stand. To illustrate the narrowing aspect of AND, add an additional search parameter to the students standing and have them sit if they meet it (up to four can be used effectively).

Tell students to pay particular attention to the power of AND as each additional AND is added. With OR, have all students stand only if they match the search criteria. This illustrates nicely how searches are "enlarged" with this operator.

27. Using an Ordinary Cookie Recipe to Illustrate Boolean Searching

Colleen Bell
University of Oregon, Eugene, Oregon

Introduction	Through lecture and active discovery, students will master the concepts of Boolean logic and will be able to formulate complex search strategies involving two or more concepts.
Subject	Any
Level of Activity	Intermediate (Students should know basic keyword searching.)
Time Required	Preparation time: 30 minutes; class time: 90 minutes
Size of Class	25 (Students are assigned to groups of five.)
Preparation	For this exercise, you will need the following items:

1. An overhead transparency showing the ingredients for a cookie recipe that includes ingredients that can be substituted (e.g., margarine for butter) and ingredients that can be excluded (nuts, raisins, etc.). The following is an oatmeal cookie recipe:

1/2 c. butter, softened	1-1/2 c. flour
1/2 t. allspice	1 c. sugar
1/2 t. baking soda	1/4 c. milk
2 eggs	1/2 t. baking powder
1 c. raisins1 t. vanilla extract	1/2 t. salt
1 c. chopped nuts	1-1/2 c. rolled oats
1 t. cinnamon	

2. Two to three overhead transparencies with blank Venn diagrams.
3. One transparency of a search strategy worksheet (Figure 27-1) and a marker for each group.
4. A list of research topics to use as examples, plus one topic for each group. Possible topics include: retention of secondary level migrant students; effects of affirmative action on men; links between cancer and personality; English as the US official language.
5. Blank transparencies.

Class Instructions

Part I (25 minutes): Divide the class into groups. Demonstrate searches that narrow (e.g., from 500 to 50 items) and ones that broaden (from 2 to 25 items). Using the cookie recipe, have students write five statements, using two ingredients and one Boolean operator. Insist that students use all three Boolean operators (AND, OR, NOT) at least once. Have students discuss how combinations might affect the resultant mixture. Examples:

1. 1/2 c. butter and 1 c. sugar: Resulting mixture does not resemble butter or sugar, but it may affect the volume.
2. 1/2 c. butter OR 1/2 c. margarine: May affect taste and texture, but not the volume.
3. 1 c. raisins NOT 1 c. nuts: Will affect the taste and may affect the volume.

Part II (15 minutes): Introduce Venn diagrams along with a research topic such as "Can one contract AIDS from mosquitoes?" Have the class decide on the two concepts in the statement, and have them generate synonyms for each concept (HIV, acquired immune deficiency syndrome, insects, etc.). Elicit search statements from the class using all three operators and write them down on the transparency.

aids AND mosquito

AIDS   mosquito

aids OR hiv

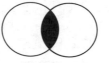

AIDS   HIV

mosquito NOT coast

mosquito   coast

Part III (50 minutes): Introduce the search strategy planner form. Have the students help you fill it out as you explain how to use it with the research topic from Part II. Students may not know the names of relevant subject indexes (e.g., MEDLINE), so have them choose the types of indexes that might be useful (e.g., a medical index, a business index). **[15 minutes]**

Distribute search topics consisting of no more than three concepts to each group. Have the students create search statements using various operators and shade in the Venn diagrams. Ask the question "If you were searching an index using this particular search statement, which part of the diagram would hold the articles or books found?" Delegate a spokesperson from each group to present the group's work. Allow time for questions. **[35 minutes]**

Discussion

This exercise can be done in two classes. End the first class with the beginning of Part III. You may also extend the exercise to include hands-on time. You may also elect to explain more advanced search techniques, such as proximity searching, truncation, field-specific searching, etc., depending on the index and retrieval software you are using.

FIGURE 27-1

SEARCH STRATEGY PLANNER

Instructions:
1. Choose the index(es) that best covers your topic.
2. Write a brief statement describing your research topic.
3. Divide the statement into concepts (i.e., main ideas). List these under Concept 1, Concept 2, etc.
4. List keywords, synonyms, related terms, and descriptors below each concept.
5. Write your search statement. Synonyms and related terms are linked together using **OR**. Concepts are linked together using **AND**. Use parentheses to group terms for each concept together [e.g., (retention OR attendance) AND migrant students].

Index(es):

_____

_____

Research Topic Statement:

_____

_____

Concepts and Terms:

CONCEPT 1 **AND**	CONCEPT 2 **AND**	CONCEPT 3
main idea:	main idea:	main idea:
terms	terms	terms
OR	**OR**	**OR**
OR	**OR**	**OR**
OR	**OR**	**OR**

Search Statement:

_____

28. Identifying LC Subject Headings and Using Boolean Operators

Stephanie Race
University of South Florida, Tampa, Florida

Introduction	This is the first of a two-part session introducing students to basic keyword searching. The second session emphasizes hands-on time searching the online catalog using what was learned in the first session. Students have already been taught author/title/subject searching and understand controlled vocabulary. (This exercise is used in a three-credit "Library Resources and Research" course but can be adapted for one or two-shot sessions.)
Subject	Any
Level of Activity	Intermediate
Time Required	60–75 minutes, depending on discussion
Size of Class	Any
Preparation	1. Librarian makes a large sheet of paper with a colored marker available to groups of three to four students. 2. Librarian photocopies exercise sheets (Figure 28-1) and distributes them to the class.
Class Instructions	1. The librarian begins by discussing successful and unsuccessful searches using LC Subject Headings. Problems in "translating" keywords and subjects to acceptable LC headings are examined here. 2. The librarian then projects a transparency containing four, color-coded research topic questions to the class. Working in groups of three or four, students are instructed to copy down the question that corresponds with the color of their markers. ("Coloring" each group allows the librarian to refer to the "blue group," "red group," etc., in the group discussion.) 3. Each research topic question consists of three concepts. Students are to identify the main ideas in each question. Each statement is

discussed. The librarian then explains why some words make good concepts while others might cause problems (e.g., vague words like *effects*).

4. After the main concepts of each question are identified, the librarian discusses the possibility of an LC heading that will describe a concept exactly. Students are asked to generate synonyms for the concepts they identified. Each concept is written side by side, with synonyms listed below. This leads to a discussion of which words are actually synonyms, versus those words that narrow the concept. The librarian encourages students to give variations of the same word.

5. The librarian uses transparencies to introduce and explain Boolean operators. Before beginning a serious discussion, the librarian asks the class to stand and "become part of a Boolean search." Have the males OR females stand. Then have the males who are (AND) fraternity members stand. Then have the females who are (AND) athletes stand. One variation might be the fraternity members who are male (AND) wear glasses stand. Then, for a bit of humor, have the people who are male AND female stand!

6. Boolean operators are explained, and examples of each type of operator are written on a transparency or blackboard. Use this time to introduce truncation and, if you have time, examples of nested search statements.

7. Students are given a homework assignment that reinforces what was presented in class (Figure 28-2).

For the next class session, students then apply this knowledge by searching the online catalog or other electronic indexes.

FIGURE 28-1
Keyword Searching

NAME_____

In order to most effectively use the capabilities of an electronic database, it is useful to use a search strategy worksheet to help organize your thoughts. A sample worksheet is attached.

Notice that the worksheet has a place for you to write out the search topic. You should be able to

DESCRIBE WHAT YOU ARE LOOKING FOR IN ONE SENTENCE.

If you cannot say what you want in one sentence, you probably need to think about it some more to get a clearer idea of what you are trying to ask.

After you have written your topic sentence, look at it and pick out the two or three main ideas (concepts) that you can give a computer to identify your topic. Ignore small words such as with, the, by, and, to, an, from, for. Each concept should be expressed in just a word or a short phrase (two or three words). List each of these concepts in the proper place on the search worksheet. For example:

Example of a ————————⟶ Locate articles on censoring the words in music.
topic sentence

	Concept 1	**Concept 2**
The two main ideas ————⟶	censoring	words in music

Not every word in the search topic becomes a concept for searching. Typically, two or three concepts (sometimes only one) will do to describe the topic without being too specific or too general. The actual number depends on your search.

1. Isolate the significant concepts in the following statements (underline or circle each concept):

   a. How is caffeine removed from beverages?

   b. What are the latest safety devices in automobiles?

   c. What animals are used for detecting drugs?

   d. What kinds of treatments are available for alcoholics?

FIGURE 28-1 cont.

Now that you have identified the important concepts, you will need to think of all of the different words that could be used to express these ideas. For instance, lyrics, music, MTV, or record album could all be used interchangeably to refer to the idea of words in music.

Just as you can use different words, you can also use different tenses and the plural or singular forms of words to express your concepts. Planning and listing all the ways that a concept might be referred to is very important. If you need help finding the right words, there are books (called thesauri) that contain suggested synonyms.

2. List below some synonyms or related terms for the sample topic.

   Topic: Locate articles on censoring the words in music.

Concept 1	Concept 2
Censoring	Words in music

Often when searching, you will want to include all variations of a word. For example, when looking for information on censor, you will also want to locate citations mentioning censoring or censored. To save yourself the trouble of entering each word separately, you may use the appropriate symbol, such as a question mark (?), as a wildcard character to locate all the variations based on the word 'censor.' For example:

          CENSOR? retrieves   CENSORS
                                      CENSORED
                                      CENSORING
                                      CENSORSHIP

This use of the ? is called **truncation** and should be planned on the worksheet. Look at the list of terms representing each concept and look for the common stem. You need to be careful, though, because truncating on a very short stem could retrieve words you don't want. For example, if you truncated the stem ban (to retrieve banned), you would retrieve records containing words like banana, band, bandages, etc.

FIGURE 28-1 cont.

3. Using one of these topic statements, list appropriate synonyms, plurals, and alternative tenses for each of the concepts.

    a. How is caffeine removed from beverages?

    b. What are the latest safety devices in automobiles?

    c. What animals are used for detecting drugs?

    d. What kinds of treatments are available for alcoholics?

Now that you have isolated your concepts and chosen your search terms, you must create relationships between each of these words; you must include in your search some way to tell the computer how the concepts are related. You do this by inserting logical operators between the concept words in your search.

There are three **logical operators** used in online searching (also called **Boolean operators**, named after George Boole, the mathematician who originated Boolean algebra). The operators are OR, AND, and NOT.

OR	The OR operator is used for synonymous terms and tells the computer that any of the search terms connected by OR can be used interchangeably, since they all refer to one concept. In the example, either lyric or words in music may be used. The information you want the computer to find can be about lyrics or words in music (or the variations of these words).
AND	The AND operator is used to intersect two or more concepts. When you use the AND operator, you require the computer to locate articles containing a combination of several different ideas. In the example, both censor and music must be used. The information you want must contain the combination of both of these ideas.
NOT	The NOT operator excludes or eliminates a particular term from the search. It is rarely used. In the example, you might want information on any kind of music but not music on videotapes.

FIGURE 28-1 cont.

As you complete your worksheet, you will determine where the logical operators will be used in your search.

Anything you list in one column represents the same idea so you will use the OR operator to tie together all the terms in that column as one concept. At the same time, each of these separate concepts are combined by using the AND operator.

You can enter search statements with two or more *different* logical operators; however, to do this you must use parentheses to separate the relationships so the computer will interpret them correctly. For example, you could combine the two statements into one statement:

(CENSOR? OR BAN OR BANNED) AND (LYRIC? OR MUSIC? OR RECORD ALBUM OR MTV)
      ^   ^   ^

      first concept   AND operator   second concept
                        joins the two
                          concepts

Notice how the parentheses are used. Each concept block, using OR relationships, is surrounded by parentheses to separate it from the AND operator. The computer processes the statement in the following order:

1st	words within parentheses
2nd	NOT relationships
3rd	AND relationships
4th	OR relationships

Search statements can become very complex. For this reason, it is a good idea to create several short OR statements and then use AND to combine the resulting sets. If you do enter complex statements with parentheses, remember to keep track of the parentheses you use: for every left parenthesis in the statement there should also be a matching right parenthesis.

4. Using one of these topic statements and the list of synonyms, plurals, and alternative tenses that you have already created, write a search statement using logical operators and parentheses to indicate the correct relationships.

    a.   How is caffeine removed from beverages?
    b.   What are the latest safety devices in automobiles?
    c.   What animals are used for detecting drugs?
    d.   What kinds of treatments are available for alcoholics?

FIGURE 28-2
Keyword Search Strategy

STEP ONE:
State your topic in one sentence: (20 points)

STEP TWO:
Analyze your topic into key concepts (ideas): (25 points)

(Terms such as "effect," "attitude," "relationship between" do not usually work as search concepts.)

CONCEPT 1	CONCEPT 2	CONCEPT 3	CONCEPT 4

STEP THREE:
Consider possible synonyms for the concepts, using a thesaurus if available: (30 points)

CONCEPT 1	CONCEPT 2	CONCEPT 3	CONCEPT 4

STEP FOUR:
Combine terms: (25 points)

(concept 1a or concept 1b) and (concept 2a or concept 2b or concept 2c) and (concept 3)

29. Selecting the "Proper" Subject Heading

Gary M. Klein
Hatfield Library, Willamette University, Salem, Oregon

Introduction

Starting with the commonly held assumption that any phrase that you think of will be the best way to search for a given subject, you will be shattering a myth and then replacing it with an easy-to-use tool. This exercise demonstrates that students can readily overcome the vagaries of language by learning how to use tools that guide them through the subject headings used to index journal articles. By taking a few moments to list some synonyms that exist within our language, students can be guided into seeing how those words are used as subject headings by indexing or abstracting tools. Students also learn how to modify the search process to increase preciseness of finding appropriate subject headings for their needs. This exercise also helps index users to gain control over their searching strategy; to narrow, broaden, or move beyond the original concept of a research topic to fit the ever-changing body of literature. This exercise uses brainstorming to develop a "shopping list" of possible subject headings. The examples shown are from sources that focus on "coping with disasters" and "disaster preparedness."

Subject

Any

Level of Activity

Intermediate to graduate level

Size of Class

Maximum 30–35 students

Time Required

Preparation: 60–90 minutes; in-class, 30 minutes

Preparation

1. Decide on a subject-oriented abstracting or indexing service appropriate for all the students in the session to work with.
2. Choose a topic appropriate to their subject interest and upcoming assignments. Example: "Coping with disasters" or "Disaster preparedness" could be used with students in business, education, engineering, or history.

The following services are among the most appropriate for this topic:

Business Periodicals Index	*Applied Science & Technology Index*
Engineering Index	*PAIS/Public Affairs Information Service*
General Science Index	*Humanities Index*
Education Index	*Historical Abstracts*
ERIC	

3. Brainstorm to come up with a specific topic as an example that you can work with in class. Use something that was recently in the headlines (e.g., forest fires, earthquakes, tornadoes, volcanic eruptions, flooding).

4. Frame the research topic into a question: "If you had to do research on natural disasters, such as earthquakes, and needed to focus on disaster preparedness and coping with disasters, what subject headings would you look up to find articles on your topic?" Make a written list of the phrases that come to mind. For example, eight phrases that might come to mind with the topic of: "Coping with and preparing for earthquake-related disasters" include:

Coping with disasters	Disaster preparedness
Earthquakes	Fault lines
Natural disasters	San Andreas Fault
Seismic activity	Plate tectonics

5. Pull out one year's worth of the index you have decided to use, and look up all of those phrases that you just jotted down in Step #4. Note which phrases are usable as is and which ones are cross-referenced. Make note of the EXACT format for each valid heading used by that index.

   Example: Using the 1995 edition of the *Applied Science & Technology Index*, you will find nothing listed under: "Coping with disasters" nor "Disaster preparedness"; 5 citations listed under "Disasters" and 7 cross-references; and over 20 related headings, many of which offer additional cross-references.

6. Make detailed notes of which subject headings were useful, either directly as is, or through their cross-references. Trace out all of the cross-references. Keep all of the punctuation intact to demonstrate the relationship between main headings and their sub-headings or related concepts.

   Cross-check and verify that each heading is actually providing access to at least one appropriate article for your topic. As you verify the reasonableness of these headings, keep adding to your list any useful cross-references that you might find.

   Example: Using the 1995 edition of the *Applied Science & Technology*

Index, you will find that there are many access points to the concept of earthquakes and disasters:

Number of citations	Usable subject headings
12	Aftershocks
6	Assistance in emergencies
23	Strike-slip faults
23	Thrust faults (Geology)

7. Type up the listing that you compiled in Step #6, incorporating the punctuation marks that identify main headings from sub-headings. Sort the listing alphabetically. Space it out so that there is plenty of room to take notes. Label the sheet with the name and volume number of the indexing/abstracting source that you used. Run off enough copies for every student in your class. Before you distribute them, fold the sheets in half, so that the outside is totally blank, then staple them shut.

8. Prepare the visual aids to accompany your presentation. Make sure that you have sufficient copies of the index or abstracting service that you are demonstrating for the students to pass around. Superseded copies of quarterly indexes are perfect for this presentation. If students will be sitting at a large conference table, you can have up to 3 students share a single volume. Alternatively, you could use an overhead projector or individual computers. Prepare an enlarged photocopy for everyone to take, so students can see all the major features of the index: actual entries on the topic; actual list of headings with their cross-references; and entries that could only be obtained by following a cross-reference.

9. It is helpful to have a variety of indexing/abstracting tools on hand that are relevant to the class that you are teaching. This will facilitate a discussion of narrow versus general coverage, and depth versus breadth of coverage, so that students can have a better understanding of the variety of subject-oriented indexes that are available.

Class Instructions

If you cannot get to a store, and your shopping list only has the word KETCHUP on it, how will someone else know if that is the same thing as CATSUP? How should you explain your shopping instructions to someone else, if you have certain preferences? For instance, you might have certain taste or brand preferences. Without having a detailed shopping list prepared in advance, how do you tell someone else what you will pay for—any brand that is extra thick, or any type of barbecue flavor—and what you will reject—anything with onions, or anything costing more than 15 cents per ounce?

Explain to the class that you are going to use a single topic for creating an example on using library resources.

Announce the sample topic and also write it on the blackboard or an overhead screen. Pass out the stapled sheets, and ask the students to spend a minute or so jotting down their suggestions for search strategies on the blank side of the paper. Pose the question: "If you had to do research on natural disasters, such as Earthquakes, and needed to focus on Disaster preparedness or Coping with disasters, what subject headings would you use to find articles?" Walk around the room and assist students in the brainstorming process.

When the students seem to be finished writing, ask them which type of index they might use to find journal articles on the topic. Might you be able to find articles in an art index? A business index? Or an education index? Shatter their myths and giggles with real-life examples.

Show them sample entries that you prepared (either a handout or on screen) from some of the less obvious sources. Hold up a copy of the actual index that the sample entry comes from. Talk about the variety of indexing and abstracting tools that are available in your library. Pass actual copies of the indexes around the room.

Ask the students if a geology index would use the same terminology as an index that is dedicated solely to art, education, or business. "Why would anyone want to turn to an art (or education or business) index to find articles about earthquakes? Have some citations in hand or displayed on a screen.

Ask students to share some of their phrases out loud with the class. They should now have a sense about which words are valid headings and which ones are likely to lead to cross-references or a dead end. If you have time, students can look up their own suggestions in their seats, or you do it selectively. Toss out a word that you know will not be usable, and get them to react to it.

Ask the class to open up their stapled sheets and compare their brainstorming list with those that you prepared in advance. Solicit comments from students who seem surprised by their findings, and go back and forth between actual indexing tools that you have on hand. This facilitates students seeing for themselves how the indexing tools can guide them in the research process. Engage students in a conversation about the physical structure of the cross-references, the SEE and SEE ALSO, the BT/NT/RT abbreviations, or whatever terminology the index uses to demonstrate conceptual relationships.

Discuss that by taking a few minutes to create a shopping list of alternative phrases (i.e., synonyms) they will spend less time in the long run looking at worthless materials. They will be able to aim for the appropriate materials faster and with more precision than ever before.

As an expansion of this exercise, if students have indexes covering different time spans, you can use that difference to demonstrate how the body of literature changes over time. If I want to look for articles on nuclear disasters, what time span is likely to have the most articles? Has anyone ever heard of Three Mile Island or Chernobyl? What years did those disasters take place? And sometimes, the words we use to describe the literature changes over time: HTLV-3, HIV, and AIDS.

Discussion   This exercise helps students to be creative in coming up with a "shopping list" of alternative subject headings (generating lists of synonyms) that will be useful for their particular research needs. The classroom activity demonstrates that an indexing/abstracting tool can guide students through the process of refining a search strategy, based on the suggestions that an index can provide to users in the form of synonyms, interrelated concepts, and alternative ways of approaching a topic. This hands-on activity also demonstrates that there are various ways to research a single topic, with each source having its own angle of coverage and relevancy.

30. Using Index Citations to Analyze Topic Change Over Time

Mary Jane Petrowski and Georgia Frank, Assistant Professor of Religion, Colgate University, Hamilton, New York

---

Introduction

This activity was devised as an alternative to a traditional term paper. Students are asked to analyze the literature on a particular topic by comparing references from two time periods, 10-20 years apart. They may also elect to compare references on the same topic in the same year in two different indexes (e.g., *Readers' Guide* and *Ethnic News Watch*). The student is introduced to the wider historical record of thinking and produces a two to three-page paper as an end product.

Subject

Any

Level of Activity

Basic

Time Required

50 minutes minimum (Two 50-minute sessions are ideal.)

Size of Class

Any

Preparation

Make copies of citations from any database on a particular topic from two years 10–20 years apart. *Readers' Guide* is recommended for this exercise. Prepare an electronic slide or overhead transparency to show citation fields.

Class Instructions

1. Students are given an identical list of citations on a particular subject from two different years in the same database.
2. In pairs, students derive strategies for analyzing the citations before doing their own analysis later. The librarian explains that scholars begin their research by trying to recognize patterns. An overhead is used to demonstrate various examples: sequences (DNA structure), cycle (bird migration, seasons), processes (converting grape juice to wine), tendencies, fads, shapes, and probabilities. Doing a literature review is presented as a way to assess what is known or thought about a subject—it's what scholars do before they design experiments, studies, or other kinds of original research. You have to know what is known before you can recognize what is not known. Another overhead showing the various fields in the citation is useful.

Give students one example by discussing author analysis. Is gender a factor? Are only men writing on this topic, etc.?

3. Students share findings while the librarian and faculty member record and discuss. The end result is a list of criteria that all students will use in doing the subsequent analysis. In a typical class, students generate between 7 and 15 analytical approaches, including: change in audience (type of magazine); increase/decrease in numbers of articles published over time; change in focus (title or abstract analysis); changes in article length (more/fewer feature-length articles); categories of change; changes in gender of authors; and increase/decrease in illustrations.

4. The librarian demonstrates online searching, and Boolean searching in particular.

5. Depending on class size, number of workstations, and topics being reviewed, students work in groups of 2, 3, or 4.

6. Students are directed to a particular database and instructed to locate and print references on the topic published at least ten years apart (e.g., 1994 and 1984; 1994 and 1974). If there are thousands or hundreds of citations in a given year, students can mark every fifth or tenth to generate a sample. One student photocopies the references for each group member. The lists are distributed to group members. (Optional: Ask students to indicate titles owned by the library.)

7. If two sessions have been allotted for this exercise, students reconvene at the second session to work in small groups, analyzing the printouts before reporting back to the class as a whole. If only one session is possible, it is important for the faculty member to reconvene the class to discuss the group findings before the written analysis is submitted.

31. Shattering the Myths of Abstracts and Indexes

Gary M. Klein
Hatfield Library, Willamette University, Salem, Oregon

Introduction	This exercise demonstrates the differences between abstracts and indexes and provides class time for students to discuss, evaluate and judge strengths and weaknesses of both tools. This exercise clearly demonstrates that abstracts and indexes are descriptive, not evaluative.
Subject	Any
Level of Activity	Basic
Time Required	30–40 minutes
Size of Class	No specific number of students required
Preparation	1. Locate an article simultaneously indexed by an indexing service and a competitor's abstracting service OR abstracted by two separate abstracting services. Examples:

> ERIC & *Psychological Abstracts*
> ERIC & *Library Literature*
> MEDLINE & *General Sciences Index*
> ABI-Inform & *Business Periodicals Index*
> ABI-Inform & *Predicasts*
> *Sociological Abstracts* & *Social Sciences Index*

2. Reformat the entries from Source #1 and Source #2 so that they are side by side on a single sheet of paper. Label all of the field headings with their full names instead of abbreviations (authors, institutional affiliation, title of article, journal name, volume number, issue number, issue date, pagination, subject headings/descriptors, abstract). Keep a copy of this sheet for yourself as a master document.

3. Working with your reformatted version of Source #1, strip out the journal name, volume number, issue number, issue date and pagination, but keep the remaining information in place. From Source #2, strip out the authors, institutional affiliation, and the title of the article. Make sure that all of the respective field headings are in their proper places after making these cuts. You may want to use different type fonts to further distinguish the two bibliographic

entries, but keep the two entries side by side on the final document. The fact that both citations refer to the same article is hidden from the students. Do not include the names of the indexes on this handout. Refer to them only as Source #1 and Source #2. This will be the basis of the classroom discussion.

4. Include sufficient space for students to make notes on the handout.
5. Photocopy and distribute this handout to students at the beginning of your session.

Class Instructions

Give students a few minutes to evaluate and compare the bibliographic information that you excerpted as Sources #1 and #2. To begin class discussion, pose the following questions:

1. Which indexing source is better? What makes it better?"
2. Of the two underlying articles that these two sources refer to, which article do you think is better? Why?
3. How might you use the information from each index source to find additional articles on the topic?
4. A final question to get students thinking about the use of subject headings should not be asked until after the class discusses the fact that both sources refer to the same journal article: "How come Source #1 and Source #2 do not use the same subject headings?"

32. Collaborative Learning Using Scientific Indexes

Christina Peterson
San Jose State University Library, San Jose, California

***

Introduction

Students will learn to use complex scientific periodical indexes in a relaxed setting with time to ask questions and seek help from the instructional librarian. Students will work in groups using a photocopied article from a zoological journal to find additional information on a topic using the authors, cited reference, subject descriptors, family, and species names as access points. The following indexes will be used:

> *Zoological Record* (in print)
> *Science Citation Index* (in print)
> *Biological Abstracts* (CD-ROM)

Subject

Zoogeography and invertebrate zoology

Level of Activity

Basic

Time Required

Preparation time: 2–3 hours; in-class, 90–120 minutes

Size of Class

Up to 25 students, in groups of 3–5

Preparation

1. Select and photocopy one article from a zoology journal for each group of 3–5 students, depending on the overall size of the class.
2. Make a transparency of the title page of each article, including the abstract.
3. Make a transparency and handouts showing the key features of each index, including a sample search and sample page or sample record.

Discussion

1. Divide students into groups of 3–5 and have them select a recorder and a reporter.
2. Distribute one article to each group.
3. Introduce the three indexes, using transparencies and handouts. **[30–40 minutes]**
4. Distribute the worksheet to each student (Figure 32-1). Ask students to brainstorm in their groups to compile keywords, species and family names, broad concepts, authors, and geographic descriptors to locate additional articles to the abstract they were given.

Have the recorder take notes about the search process and jot down references to useful articles. **[30–40 minutes]**

5. Circulate among the groups while they complete the worksheets to answer specific questions about each index used.

6. Ask the reporter from each group to explain which keywords, concepts, etc., the group extracted from the abstract to use as search possibilities. Ask the reporter if there were any problems with the search, and ask the entire class to provide suggestions for solutions. **[30–40 minutes]**

FIGURE 32-1
Student Worksheet

GOAL: Find journal papers related to your group's given paper.

CHOOSE: A **recorder** to take notes on the steps outlined below.
A **reporter** to present your findings to the class.
STEPS:

1. Analyze your group's paper.

    Author(s):

    Topics and keywords:

    Species:

    Broad taxonomic groups (class, family, etc.):

2. Use *Zoological Record* to find more papers. What *Zoological Record* index(es) did you use?

    _____ author   _____ subject   _____ geographical   _____ species

List one or more journal papers **in English** related to your given paper.

3. Use *Science Citation Index* to find related papers. Which section(s) of *Science Citation Index* did you use?
    _____ source   _____ citation   _____ permuterm

List one or more papers **in English** related to your given paper.

4. Use *Biological Abstracts on CD ROM* to find more papers. What keywords and concept codes did you use?

List one or more papers **in English** related to your given paper.

5. Compare and contrast the three sources for **ease of use** and **range of information**. Which will you use first when you research your paper for this course?

33. Using Multiple Information Sources

Diane Prorak
University of Idaho Library, Moscow, Idaho

Introduction

Many classes need to learn several different information sources during a single library session. During this exercise, students working in small groups examine a specific information resource. At the end of the exercise, each group introduces and demonstrates the resource they examined. Finally, the librarian demonstrates how to find out whether the library owns the periodicals containing needed articles. If time permits, demonstrate some statistical and Internet sources.

Subject

Any

Level of Activity

Basic

Time Required

in class: approximately one hour

Size of Class

15–30

Preparation

1. Develop a brief "canned" demonstration of the online catalog and indexes and abstracts, including parts of a citation and the function of abstracts.
2. Photocopy "Index Exploration and Evaluation" exercise sheets (Figure 33-1) for each relevant information resource (one sheet per group). NOTE: These sheets will have to be customized to indicate indexes to be used and locations.
3. Prepare live demonstration of how to determine if the library owns a periodical. If time permits, demonstrate the use of a statistical source.

Class Instructions

1. Pick an index you would like to explore. It will be to your advantage to pick an index with which you are not familiar.
2. Go to a workstation or an area where this source can be found.
3. Provide the information requested on the exercise sheet.
4. After your group has finished, come back to the classroom.
5. (Each group in turn.) Please come to the front of the class to demonstrate and discuss the index or abstract your group explored.

6. Demonstrate how to find out whether the library owns the periodical containing the article. Mention that articles not in the library's collection can be retrieved through interlibrary loan.
7. OPTIONAL: If time permits, show examples of useful statistical and Internet resources.

Discussion

This exercise requires two separate mini-lectures: (1) the distinction between catalogs and indexes/abstracts and (2) the process of locating and retrieving articles found in the index search, in statistical information, and from Internet resources. The first mini-lecture, and most of the second, can be prepared in advance using presentation software such as PowerPoint to illustrate necessary resources and features. It is recommended that article retrieval be performed live and that a citation from one of the groups be used as an example.

With large classes, statistical and Internet components should have their own worksheets and be assigned to groups, rather than relying on demonstration from the librarian.

FIGURE 33-1

INDEX EXPLORATION AND EVALUATION

1. Name of index or abstract:

2. Location in the library or means of access:

3. Scope
   a.   Subjects covered:

   b.   Type of publications included:

   c.   Years covered:

4. Does this have a thesaurus or subject list you could use? If so, where is this list located?

5. Each person in the group should try to look up the topic for their paper in the index. Copy down the citation to one article below. Your group should be ready to demonstrate and explain to the class how you found this item. Copy down the following information (or print it out):
   - Author:
   - Title:
   - Title of journal (if applicable):
   - Date:
   - Volume of journal (if applicable):
   - Pages:

6. Are there summary abstracts included with the citations for articles?

7. Mention any problems or any special features you encountered as you used this index.

Section III

Search Strategies for the Research Process

Edited by Gail Gradowski and Loanne Snavely

We are all too familiar with the typical quick-and-dirty search strategy employed by the average undergraduate. It is characterized by a desire to, above all, save time. As such, there is a real horror of ever having to double back or rethink or start over. Furthermore, that hurrying discourages, even forbids, any reflection or experimentation or deliberation. Certainly, there is no time to critique one's strategy!

The exercises in this chapter all encourage students to think about their search process and, therefore, about their own search strategies.

One exercise, The Case of Kelly, actually has students working in groups critique a model of a student, Kelly, doing research. Any one of them, needless to say, could be Kelly!

Two exercises deal with the very tough initial strategic step of formulating a research topic. Modeling Topic Selection is a very basic class/group discussion exercise that introduces students to some techniques they could use to focus a broad topic. It could be adapted to virtually any size class. The design entitled Think-Pair-Share can work on a variety of levels as well as with a variety of class sizes. It is also a very nice opportunity to try out this very basic active learning technique.

Another exercise focuses on the flow of information, relating information to time and then to types of sources. The Information Trail uses current events for its examples, but it could be modified to other specific topic areas.

Last, but not least, is an exercise that in very large part is derived directly from specific student concerns/needs/anxieties. This is Understanding Research as a Creative Process. It can be used as a 15-minute starter in a longer session and, because it is based on the immediate needs of a specific set of students, is very flexible with regards to discipline and level. The author also suggests some ways to use this exercise to segue into other discussions and further exercises. If you want to see how Carol Kuhlthau's Model of the Research Process can be used in a class session, be sure to take a look at this one.

34. The Case of Kelly

Denise Madland and Carol Hagness
University of Wisconsin-Stout, Menomonie, Wisconsin

Introduction

This activity was designed for use in first-year composition classes coming to the library to learn to use the online catalog and indexes and to develop search strategies in preparation for writing their research papers, usually on any topic of their choice. Some classes have been introduced to basics through two slide-tape presentations with accompanying exercises, while others have no preparation beforehand. This activity works in both situations.

Through the use of a case study about Kelly's search for information in the library, students, in small groups, are asked to evaluate Kelly's search strategy and are then given an opportunity to share their knowledge and discover new strategies and sources for finding information. If computer terminals are available, the students can try out some of the searches they have developed and compare the differences in retrieval. The activity highlights the importance of search strategy and leads into evaluation of sources. It also puts students in a participatory frame of mind and includes them in the discovery process.

Subject

Any

Level of Activity

Basic

Time Required

Preparation time (first time only), 1 hour; in class, 10–15 minutes (first part), 10–12 minutes (second part)

Size of Class

10–30 students

Preparation

1. Adapt "The Case of Kelly" (Figure 34-1) to your library and desired topic and photocopy for each student in the class.
2. Adapt the summary to your library and create an overhead transparency. (You could also create this part on the board during the class discussion.)

**Class Instructions/
Discussion**

Part I

Divide students into groups of two, three, four, or five, depending on how many students are in the class and where they have chosen to sit.

Pass out a copy of "The Case of Kelly" to each student. Ask them to read it and to discuss the questions at the end with their group. Ask them to select one person from their group to act as the recorder of the results of the discussion. Also request that when finished with the questions, they turn over their papers and brainstorm keywords that might be used to search for this topic. During the group discussions, it is important to circulate among the groups and help get everyone involved.

When they are done, begin a discussion by asking each group to name one mistake, and so on for each question. The discussion can take a variety of routes, depending on the responses.

Using the points brought up in the discussion, and the keywords generated by the brainstorming, work with the class to develop a preferred search strategy. This can be summed up on a prepared overhead transparency or written on the board as it unfolds.

Part II (Optional—requires workstations in or near the classroom)

After examining Library of Congress Subject Headings (through the use of the transparencies) and developing a variety of potentially useful keyword combinations, have the groups try different search statements at their terminals, ask them to compare the number of hits produced with their search statement. If time allows, have them examine some of the citations retrieved. Ask them if they think their search statement produced relevant information. Have the groups read one or two of the best titles they found. Which keyword combinations seemed to produce the best results. Why?

FIGURE 34-1

THE CASE OF KELLY

Kelly decided to do her paper on hiring of minorities in the workplace. Many of her classes had been talking about the value of diversity and a multicultural work force. She didn't really understand which groups of people were considered minorities, or what issues were involved. She proceeded to the second floor of the library to look for the most recent issues of *Newsweek*, hoping to find an article or two. Not finding anything, she remembered that her teacher had talked about the periodical *Business Week*. She looked at the current issue and found articles on employment, but nothing on minorities. She talked a friend into helping her find the older issues on paper copy and microfiche. They browsed for two hours and still didn't find anything useful. Time for lunch at the Student Center.

After lunch Kelly returned to the library, passed the smiling reference librarian and headed for the public catalog. Surely she could find a book on employee hiring. Yes, this one looked good, *Hiring Valuable Employees*, by A. J. Mayer, Prentice-Hall, 1972. Best news yet, it had a bibliography! Maybe she could get some other information sources from the bibliography.

Before going upstairs for the book, Kelly decided to stop by *World Book Encyclopedia*. Her friend had said it was at the back of the Reference Room. She could probably rely on it for a lot of information about minorities.

QUESTIONS

1. Did Kelly make any errors in trying to find information? If so, what were they?

2. What are the good points of her search?

3. Were the information sources Kelly used appropriate? Why, or why not?

4. What other sources would you have used, or what would you have done differently?

35. Modeling Topic Selection

Esther Grassian
Los Angeles College Library, University of California

Introduction

This is a three part exercise designed to aid students in understanding how a topic is formulated. The third part is optional. The librarian models the process of selecting a topic, defining the parameters with input from the students and creating a topic sentence.

Next the students work in small groups with a different broad topic provided by the librarian, and a comparison is made of each group's results. In the third part students work individually on two additional topics of their choice. After participating in this activity, students have often visibly relaxed about the process of selecting a topic and doing research on it, and it's fun. The hardest part is making sure that the topic you model is both broad enough and current enough to get their attention.

Subject

Any

Level of Activity

Basic

Time Required

Part I: 5 minutes or less; Part II: about 10 minutes; Part III: 5 minutes

Size of Class

This exercise is used for classes of about 25, but it would work for much larger classes as well. The only difference would be that not every group would be able to report back because of the time constraints.

Class Instructions/ Discussion

Part I

Begin by modeling topic selection in the following way:
1. Write a broad topic on the board—e.g., Terrorism—and explain that you will show the students four means of narrowing or broadening a topic.
2. Write the word "Time" on the board and ask the rhetorical question: "Am I interested in 'terrorism' from the beginning of time to the present, or do I have a specific time period in mind?" The answer of course is, yes, I have a specific time period in mind, so pick a time period or range of dates, or compare two time periods—e.g., 1965–1985—and write it on the board.

3. Write the word "Place" on the board, and ask a similar rhetorical question about geographic region. Pick a region and write it on the board following the word "place"—e.g., Israel

4. Write the words "Person or Group" on the board, and again, ask a rhetorical question about focus on individual or group. Pick a person or group and write it one the board following the words "person or group"—e.g., city dwellers.

5. Write the words "Event or Aspect" on the board, ask a similar rhetorical question about it. Pick an event or aspect and write it on the board—e.g., fear of attack

6. Have a topic sentence ready and write it on the board—e.g., "Did fear of terrorist attack increase or decrease among city dwellers in Israel from 1965 to 1985?"

7. Explain that this may or may not be a researchable topic, but that's the way research is done—you come up with a topic and then broaden, narrow or delete one or more of the four parameters (time, place, person/group, event/aspect) as you look for information on a topic.

Part II

Next, tell the class that you will break them into small groups, give them all a broad topic (different from the one you modeled), and give them 5 minutes to come up with 1–4 limiters and a topic sentence. Remind them that they do not necessarily have to use all 4 limiters.

After 5 minutes, ask groups to report back to the entire class, reading off their limiters and their topic sentences. Call the class's attention to the fact that each group came up with different (or somewhat different) topic sentences and limiters—i.e., there are lots of ways to define a topic..

Part III (optional)

Ask each individual student to work through this process for 2 additional topics of their choice and turn them in to the instructor. The instructor may then select one of them for the student to develop into a paper or return it for further refinement.

36. Think-Pair-Share for Topic Formulation

Necia Parker-Gibson
Mullins Library, University of Arkansas, Fayetteville, Arkansas

---

Introduction

The objective of this exercise is to help students generate elements that make a topic a good one and see why some subjects will not work. Use it when students are having a hard time choosing or developing topics for short term papers.

Subject

Any

Level of Activity

First-year students up to graduate level

Time Required

10–12 minutes (Allow more time the first time you try it.)

Size of Class

20–40 students

Preparation

1. Talk with the instructor, who will let you know if the students are having trouble finding appropriate topics. Get the details of the assignment orally, an assignment sheet, or both.
2. Think about the assignment and the elements that would make a term paper topic fit the assignment. Generate ideas before the class and remember to be flexible. The students are likely to surprise you, one way or the other.
3. Be prepared to feel uncertain. Any new exercise is a risk. The students seem to really like this one, and the instructors are grateful to have the students assisted in this process. (It results in fewer last-minute calls to them!)

Class Instructions

1. Introduce yourself and the library in a general way before you get into the topics problem. It is a good way to begin a class, because once they have some ideas for topics, they seem to listen more carefully. They have started to become involved in the process.
2. Hand out 3x5 index cards or scrap paper for the students to write ideas on. It does not hurt to have some golf pencils available, too!
3. Tell them that you will give them:
   • Two minutes to think about what makes a good term paper topic (Start them off with some general ideas—you want them to think in terms of depth, currency, relevance, etc.) and write them down.

- Three minutes to discuss what they jotted down with their immediate neighbor (if there are odd numbers of students, use one group of three).

4. Take the elements that they agree on from each pair or group and write them on the board or a transparency. Briefly discuss the elements that you write, but wait until all have submitted their ideas to comment on them.

5. Use open-ended questions like these to lead the discussion in ways you want to go:
   - Why would this be a good/easy topic?
   - Is it possible to have an easy topic that is not a good topic? How? Why?
   - What do you need to research this topic?
   - How much can you rely on your own knowledge for this topic/ this paper?
   - Are your friends a good or a bad source of information compared to published sources?

Discussion

If the students are offering you actual topics as opposed to giving you ideas for the parameters of a good topic, then you must give guidance without being too critical in front of their peers. If they see you generate a reasonable topic and break it down by its relevance, appropriate focus, researchability in the allotted time, and so on, then they get the idea faster.

Students enjoy this exercise and listen to the research/library skills lecture better afterwards. It also gives the librarian an idea of where they stand in relation to library research. Many of them are terribly naive. It gets them involved in some group learning in a relatively non-threatening, painless way and helps enlist the kinesthetic learners, the auditory learners and the visual learners in the process.

The pairing has not been much of a problem, because there are no "wrong" answers and the exercise is not intimate enough to be a problem between acquaintances. There can be a little trouble in getting them quiet for the lecture demonstration afterward, but if you can show how a good topic works in the catalog and the indexes, you can move into it without too much delay. The instructor can help with this, too.

37. The Information Trail: Tracking Current Events

Allison Level
Library of Congress, Washington, D.C.

Introduction

You read about it in the newspaper, or see it on the evening news, but what information really comes out about a current event, action, tragedy, or triumph?. In this activity, students work with a specific current event or activity and track information about that topic. With this exercise, it is also possible to look at different information-seeking roles as they pertain to the topic.

OBJECTIVES:
• Provide students with an understanding of the timeframe for information dissemination
• Direct students to using multiple sources and formats for seeking information on a topic
• Provide students with an understanding of different information-seeking roles

Subject

Any current event related to the course subject (e.g., an earthquake or volcanic eruption for a geology or science class)

Level of Activity

Basic (Can be modified to use intermediate or advanced concepts)

Time Required

Preparation, 1–2 hours; in-class, 1–3 hours

Size of Class

10–50 students (Divide a large class into groups of 4–8)

Preparation

Determine the length of the class and the level of activity you want to cover. For a 50–60 minute class, the basic activity level is best. Brainstorm a list of current events, or match the events based on the class topic, or time of year. Try to select interesting events for the class or group you are working with, and use a timeframe that allows for good information coverage. If you have lots of smaller groups and a limited amount of time, you can assign the same topic to several groups, but have each group look at different formats or sources.

Create a list of possible sources for information. Do your own search in some of these sources in advance to have actual examples in hand for the class. Review any information-seeking roles you would want the students to cover. It is not necessary, but it might be helpful to prepare a worksheet for students to use during the exercise (See Figure 37-1).

Class Instructions

Welcome to the Information Trail. Your assignment today is to track a current event or current topic and examine the types of information available about that topic, the different sources that provide information, who is writing about the topic, and the different formats possible for finding information about the topic.

You and your group will follow this event through a specific timeframe and locate information that may be of interest to different types of people. As you work, pay attention to the following questions:

- What kind of information is available about this topic (e.g., general information, specific, technical)?
- How long did it take for information to come out about this topic?
- At what point did information become readily available? Has information on the topic been difficult to locate?
- What different kinds of sources are helpful in locating information on the topic?
- Is information available in various formats? Are some formats more helpful than others?

You can also step into the shoes of someone seeking information about this topic. If you were a news reporter, government official, parent, or research scientist, how would your information needs be different?

Discussion

The discussion can focus on the "process" of the research, how easy or hard it was to find information, what kind of information was available, and how long the dissemination process took. Discussion can also follow the information-seeking roles. Does who you are make a difference in what you what to know?

You can also use the results of this exercise to talk with students about evaluating sources of information, primary vs. secondary sources of information, and the impact of electronic access and the Internet on information dissemination.

FIGURE 37-1
Sample Worksheet Outline

Name of topic or event:

Timeframe for seeking information about the topic:

Information-seeking role (if any):

For each source you use, please answer the following:

• What is the source? Include its title, call number, location, or URL.

• What information was found using this source?

• What was the timeframe for information provided by this source?

• Did this source refer you to other resources?

• How helpful was this source?

• Did you find information you did not expect to find?

• If so, what was it? Add your own additional comments.

• Which sources did you find the most helpful? Why?

• Which sources provided little information? Why?

Other comments or questions that came up during the exercise:

38. Understanding Research as a Creative Process

Mary Jane Petrowski
Colgate University, Hamilton, New York

Introduction	This format is a way to address a wide array of student concerns/anxieties in a very positive way. It revolves around very specific student-generated questions. As such, it is very spontaneous!
Subject	Any
Level of Activity	Probably not beginners; need to have done research before. Students also need to be immediately faced with a research assignment.
Time Required	15 minutes
Size of Class	Used in classes with up to 40.
Preparation	Need to have an overhead with Kuhlthau's (1988) research process and be familiar with cluster analysis. May need to provide students with small pieces of paper to write on.
Class Instructions	Begin the session by saying that you would like to tailor today's class to their immediate concerns about the paper and need some input to begin.

Instruct everyone to take a few minutes and write down their biggest anxiety or concern about this research project. Ask them to also indicate how many research papers they have done and how long they think it will take to complete the research for this particular paper. Be sure to tell them that their answers are anonymous.

Have a student or the instructor collect the slips and read them out loud as you create a cluster analysis on an overhead of Kuhlthau's research process (see figure 19-1). For example, if a student writes that he is worried that interlibrary loan doesn't work fast enough, I put a dot under the fifth stage, Information Collection. If someone says that they don't know how to find a topic, I put a dot under stage two, and so forth. It is easy to see where concerns are clustered just by looking at the dots under each stage. I'm always surprised by how many involve "prefocus/focus exploration."

This brief interaction generates an immediate snapshot of where the class is and what they are concerned about and gives you a framework for structuring the ensuing discussion. Students are usually amazed to see that everyone in the class is uptight and anxious about the assignment and the faculty member is invariably dumbfounded by the very basic things that worry students.

Next, you can segue into one/some/all of the following discussions:

1. Find a Pattern.
Much of what is called "intelligence" is our ability to recognize patterns. We recognize sequences (DNA structure), cycles (bird migrations), processes (how to convert grape juice into wine), tendencies, fads, shapes, and probabilities. (see figure 19-2, Von Oech, 1989

2. Research as a Process
Premise: students do not understand research as a process, particularly as a creative process involving time for reflection and gestation. Kuhlthau's model of the information search process is introduced (overhead) and discussed. The creative but difficult stages of prefocus exploration and focus formulation are highlighted along with strategies for working through those stages.

This is where you can address some of the very unrealistic research plans. Many students indicate that they plan to invest 1-2 hours researching a 30-page paper. In going through the six stages, I address the specific questions students have raised.

3. Review Research Strategies for Prefocus Exploration
Reference is made to handouts where particular reference resources, article databases and web resources are listed. Emphasize that "berry picking" or "trolling the databases" are extremely important initial activities in the exploration process.

4. Collective Online Demo
At this point you can begin an online demonstration of a particular database but ask students to direct the search. They must suggest topics and then search refinements. You can help out.

Discussion

This activity works best at the beginning of an 80-minute class when students have a major research paper assignment. It is an eye-opener for both students and faculty.

REFERENCES

Kuhlthau, C. C. (1988). Developing a model of the library search process: cognitive and affective aspects. *RQ* 28, 232–42.

Von Oech, R. (1989). *Creative Whack Pack*. Stamford, Conn.: U. S. Games Systems.

Section IV

Evaluation of Library Resources

Edited by Michael Blake and Ed Tallent

As increasing amounts of information and resources are made available to students, as resources become more easily accessible, it is incumbent upon students to learn to evaluate what they are finding. We can add to this mix the ingredient of increasing remote use, meaning a reference librarian is probably far away. While it is true that students should have been critically evaluating information resources all along, students notoriously follow the path of least resistance. The reality today is that it is easier for students to take this path to locate materials.

The goal of this section is to give instruction librarians some easy-to-follow plans to get students to think about their research needs, to imagine what kinds of resources would fill that need, to learn about the types of reference sources available to assist them, and to teach students techniques for asking good questions when evaluating resources. The examples in this chapter are instructive in that they outline how instruction librarians can focus a session around a critical thinking component. Most students have found the size and complexity of academic libraries to be intimidating, and this will not change. Students can easily be overwhelmed with too much information, but we can help by enabling them to focus and evaluate that information. Today as in the past, less is more.

Several of the examples emphasize the need to determine what class of periodical literature is needed, and then evaluating the resources eventually located. At the other end of the spectrum is the bibliography, those magic bullets (or as one of our contributors says, the "tail that wags the paper") compiled separately or as supporting documentation for research. It is crucial even with these sources that students learn to discern the perspective of the compiler(s), as well as the goals and parameters of the publication. More recently, with the explosion of WWW resources and access, a whole new universe of challenges has emerged for instruction librarians. What is striking about the examples included here is that the same approach and skills development are operative in this new world.

39. Article Citation Evaluation: A Research Process Framework

Keith Gresham
University of Colorado at Boulder

Introduction

This multi-part lesson consists of a series of collaborative, small-group exercises designed to teach the journal article research process to beginning or intermediate writing students in any academic discipline. The lesson recognizes that to successfully engage in the research process, students must first understand the concepts of research article, periodical index, article citation, and citation elements. Through an analytical and evaluative examination of article citations followed by hands-on practice with electronic periodical indexes, students discover how the citation can be used to discriminate and choose among the wide range of sources they encounter. Although the process worksheet handout used during the hands-on component of the session is designed for use with the OCLC FirstSearch online system, the worksheet can be modified for use with any individual or set of periodical indexes.

Subject

Any

Level of Activity

Undergraduate

Time Required

Preparation, 8–14 hours for handouts; in class, two 50 minute sessions

Size of Class

36 maximum

Preparation

1. Select and copy a research article for each group.
2. Adapt Figures 39-1 through 39-5 and photocopy for each student.
3. Develop a search strategy demonstrating the basic commands of FirstSearch.

Class Instructions

1. Divide the students into groups composed of 3 or 4 individuals.
2. Each group is given a sample research article to examine. Using Figure 39-1, each group is asked to decide what type of periodical the article came from and to list the elements or characteristics of the article that led the group to make its decision. A spokesperson from each group is asked to share one or two items from the group's list.

3. Using Figure 39-2, students are asked to examine the structure, organization, and purpose of a citation and to identify the type of information a citation can provide.

4. Within their small groups, students are given a hypothetical research topic and six citations to different periodical articles (Figure 39-3). Each group is asked to examine the information contained in all six citations, evaluate the appropriateness of each citation for the research topic, and choose one or two citations that seem most useful as a potential research source. In turn, each group reports on a citation it did not select and provides the reasons why the citation was not chosen.

5. Each student is given Figure 39-4, "Locating Articles using FirstSearch." Students are asked to write down topics, identify appropriate academic disciplines, choose applicable FirstSearch databases, develop a list of search vocabulary, and organize search words.

6. Sitting at computer terminals, students are walked through the process of logging onto FirstSearch and given a brief explanation of the online system (Figure 39-5). Using their individual topics, students are guided through the remainder of the search process, using Figure 39-4.

FIGURE 39-1
TYPES OF PERIODICALS

	RESEARCH JOURNALS	POPULAR MAGAZINES	NEWSPAPERS
Examples	Sociological Review Journal of Asian Studies Journal of Youth and Adolescence Social Forces	Time Newsweek Sports Illustrated U.S. News and World Report	New York Times Washington Post Wall Street Journal Denver Post
Value and Uses	Reports of original research In-depth analysis of topics Lengthy articles Statistical information	Current events and news Brief, factual information Short articles Interviews	News stories Current information Local and regional focus Analysis and opinion of current events
Language	College-level writing and vocabulary Specialized language of the discipline	Non-technical vocabulary Often simple language	Non-technical vocabulary written for a general, educated audience
Authors	Researchers, academics, scholars	Journalists	Journalists
Sources	Footnotes and bibliographies Documentation often extensive	Original sources can be obscure	Sources are rarely cited in full
Publishers	Professional organizations, universities, research institutes, and scholarly presses	Commercial/trade publisher	Commercial/trade publisher
Graphics	Graphs, charts, and tables Ads are very rare	Many graphics and photos Many full-page color ads	Photos, graphics, and charts Many ads

FIGURE 39-2
Sample Article Citation

ERIC NO: EJ467151
AUTHOR: Aguirre, Adalberto, Jr.; And Others
TITLE: Majority and Minority Faculty Perceptions in Academe.
YEAR: 1993
SOURCE: Research in Higher Education (v34 n3 p371–85 Jun 1993)
PUB TYPE: Research/technical report; Journal article
LANGUAGE: English
ABSTRACT: A study at the University of Colorado compared minority (n=73) and white (n=122) faculty perceptions of employment/workplace issues and minority affairs. Minority faculty were dissatisfied with certain contexts in the institution and felt excluded. Interactions of race and gender were also examined. (Author/MSE)
NOTES: UMI
MAJOR DESC: College Faculty; Faculty College Relationship; Job Satisfaction; Racial Differences; Teacher Attitudes; Work Environment
MINOR DESC: College Environment; Comparative Analysis; Higher Education; Minority Groups; Nontraditional Occupations; Sex Differences
IDENTIFIERS: University of Colorado

FIGURE 39-3
Sample Topic and Citations

EVALUATING CITATIONS
Small Group Exercise

GOAL: Evaluate article citations in relation to the stated paper topic.

PAPER TOPIC: Reasons why, after twelve years of AIDS prevention programs, large percentages of American teenagers continue to engage in unprotected sex.

INSTRUCTIONS: Examine the information elements contained in each of the following six article citations. As a group, evaluate each citation as to the article's usefulness or appropriateness as a research source for the paper topic. After evaluating each citation, decide which one citation the group finds to be the most useful or appropriate. Be prepared to report the group's findings, including why certain citations were not chosen.

QUESTIONS TO ANSWER:
- What type of information is needed? What type of information is appropriate for the topic?
- Is the information given in the title or summary of the article understandable?
- How well or in what ways does the article pertain to the topic?
- In which type of periodical did the article appear (newspaper, magazine, research journal)?
- How current is the information? Does currency of information matter for the topic?

CITATION 1
(TI) TITLE: AIDS and Adolescence; Sida et Adolescence
(AU) AUTHOR(S): Frappier,-Jean-Yves; Roy,-Elise; Girard,-Marc; Charbonneau,-Louise
(JN) JOURNAL NAME: Sante-mentale-au-Quebec; 1992, 17, 1, spring, 265-276.
(LA) LANGUAGE: French
(PY) PUBLICATION YEAR: 1992
(AB) ABSTRACT: Epidemiological data on HIV/AIDS (human immunodeficiency virus/acquired immune deficiency syndrome)-infected adolescents & data on the prevalence of risk behaviors among adolescents in Quebec are discussed based on existing research. While information on seropositive adolescents is scant, this population is deemed vulnerable due to risk behaviors, eg, early sexual activity, frequent change of partners, anal sex, concealed homosexuality, & substance abuse. Future tendencies are discussed with regard to three groups: (1) well-informed adolescents with few risk behaviors, with small projected infection risk; (2) homosexual adolescents, with elevated infection risk; & (3) abused or neglected adolescents with troubled family & social background who are less informed & engage in highly risky behaviors, & are therefore faced with high infection risk. Intervention methods for early detection are discussed. 17 References. Adapted from the source document. (Copyright 1993, Sociological Abstracts, Inc., all rights reserved.)

FIGURE 39-3 cont.

CITATION 2

(TI) TITLE: Adolescent Coping Behavior when Confronted with a Friend with AIDS

(AU) AUTHOR(S): Brown,-Larry-K.; Spirito,-Anthony; Reynolds,-Lyn-Ann; Hemstreet,-A

(JN) JOURNAL NAME: Journal-of-Adolescence; 1992, 15, 4, Dec, 467–477.

(LA) LANGUAGE: English

(PY) PUBLICATION YEAR: 1992

(AB) ABSTRACT: The Kidcope measure was used to compare the coping strategies employed by 1,343 US adolescents in grades 8–10 when presented with a hypothetical situation of a friend with AIDS (acquired immune deficiency syndrome) vs a friend who had attempted suicide; the impact of gender & level of distress on coping style was also assessed. A wide range of responses that were generally adaptive was reported, with girls & distressed students more likely to endorse adaptive coping items. Among friends of attempted suicides, more distress was reported by boys contrary to expectations. Overall, however, more distress & a wider variety of coping strategies were reported in response to the AIDS scenario than to the suicide problem. Implications for care of adolescents dealing with these issues are discussed. 3 Tables, 26 References. Adapted from the source document. (Copyright 1993, Sociological Abstracts, Inc., all rights reserved.)

CITATION 3

(TI) TITLE: AIDS/HIV Knowledge Level and Perceived Chance of Having HIV among Rural Adolescents

(AU) AUTHOR(S): DuRant,-Robert-H.; Ashworth,-Carolyn-Seymore; Newman,-Cheryl-L.; McGill,-Linda; Rabun,-Cindy; Baranowski,-Tom

(JN) JOURNAL NAME: Journal-of-Adolescent-Health; 1992, 13, 6, Sept, 499-505.

(LA) LANGUAGE: English

(PY) PUBLICATION YEAR: 1992

(AB) ABSTRACT: As AIDS/HIV (acquired immune deficiency syndrome/human immunodeficiency virus) emerges as a significant health problem among minority rural adolescents in the southern US, the Centers for Disease Control's 1989 Secondary School Health Risk Survey was administered to 294 junior-high school students in GA. Although 68% of the respondents (Rs) reported having received school-based AIDS/HIV education, their knowledge level was lower than national standards, particularly among younger Rs & minorities. Behavioral changes & the degree of worry about HIV exposure were more prevalent among older Rs & those receiving AIDS education. Perceived risk of having AIDS was associated with grade level, worry about HIV exposure, & AIDS/HIV knowledge. Results suggest that these rural youth, selected from areas with substantial social & health problems, not only lack adequate knowledge about AIDS/HIV risk, but also hold beliefs that could lead to increased risk of exposure. 5 Tables, 37 References. Adapted from the source document. (Copyright 1994, Sociological Abstracts, Inc., all rights reserved.)

FIGURE 39-3 cont.

CITATION 4

AUTHOR: Ingrassia, Michele.

TITLE: Virgin cool.

SOURCE: Newsweek   v. 124 (Oct. 17 '94) p. 58–62+ il.

STANDARD NO: 0028-9604

DATE: 1994

RECORD TYPE: art

CONTENTS: feature article

ABSTRACT: Among teenagers, sexual abstinence is gaining new respect. The trend follows a decades-long explosion in births among unmarried teens and a growing number of AIDS cases among young adults. Eugene Genovese, scholar-in-residence at the University Center in Georgia and an observer of campus life for 25 years, calls the abstinence movement "a broadbased counterattack against the counter-culture that developed since the 1960s." The article discusses the roles in the abstinence movement of parents, teachers, pop culture, changing attitudes about abortion, and the Christian right. Several teenagers discuss their decisions to delay sex, and statistics on teenage sexuality and abstinence are presented.

SUBJECT: Sexual abstinence.

CITATION 5

(TI) TITLE: Confronting the Challenge of AIDS among Adolescents: Directions for Future Research

(AU) AUTHOR(S): DiClemente,-Ralph-J.

(JN) JOURNAL NAME: Journal-of-Adolescent-Research; 1993, 8, 2, Apr, 156-166.

(LA) LANGUAGE: English

(PY) PUBLICATION YEAR: 1993

(AB) ABSTRACT: Reviews research issues in the battle to combat the acquired immune deficiency syndrome (AIDS) crisis in adolescents, focusing on: (1) risk of AIDS & human immunodeficiency virus (HIV) infection in culturally differing populations, particularly among African Americans; (2) empirical investigation of variables influencing adolescent HIV preventive behavior; & (3) the development of more effective prevention programs & behavior modification interventions. Specific policy recommendations include funding for basic behavioral surveys of adolescent risk-taking behavior, separation of research from political agendas, evaluation of risk-reduction interventions, & study of cultural & gender-role differences related to risk reduction behavior & HIV prevention. 43 References. Adapted from the source document. (Copyright 1994, Sociological Abstracts, Inc., all rights reserved.)

FIGURE 39–3 cont.

CITATION 6

(TI) TITLE: Knowledge about AIDS

(AU) AUTHOR(S): Taylor,-A.-J.-W.; Walkey,-F.-H.; Oude-Alink,-P.-C.

(JN) JOURNAL NAME: Health-Promotion; 1988, 3, 4, 407-411.

(LA) LANGUAGE: English

(PY) PUBLICATION YEAR: 1988

(AB) ABSTRACT: Earlier research on knowledge of AIDS (acquired immune deficiency syndrome) among the general population in New Zealand (Arnold, B., Public Knowledge of AIDS, thesis, Wellington: Victoria U, 1987) is extended in a larger study of a sample of 531 New Zealand students ages 15-20, modifying the earlier telephone questionnaire for written administration to groups. Rating 5 issues of greatest importance to them, 449 respondents (Rs) ranked AIDS fourth, & 94% of these considered it a very or fairly serious problem. In responses regarding knowledge about AIDS, the level of accuracy ranged from 67.1% to 95.4%; however, scores on knowledge of symptoms of the disease & of groups at risk were low. Although 81.5% of the Rs indicated they needed to know more about AIDS, 20% could not name a single source of information. Overall, results confirmed earlier findings of a significant aware-ness of AIDS among the most educated, but notable gaps in knowledge were still evident; implications for health education are discussed. 1 Table, 1 Appendix, 7 References. S. Dilts (Copyright 1991, Socio-logical Abstracts, Inc., all rights reserved.)

FIGURE 39-4
LOCATING ARTICLES USING FirstSearch

Topic:_____

Which academic discipline(s) does your topic fall into? _____

STEP 1: List the FirstSearch periodical indexes that are appropriate for your research subject or topic.

_____

_____

STEP 2: Write down nouns and noun phrases that describe all of the major ideas within your topic.

_____

STEP 3: Organize the nouns and noun phrases into groups based on ideas or concepts. FirstSearch allows you to use the connecting words **AND** and **OR** to narrow or expand your search.

STEP 4: Conduct your search in one of the FirstSearch periodical indexes you listed in STEP 1. Example:

SEARCH WORD(S) (or Action):   su: sexual harassment and college students

STEP 5: Evaluate your search results. Write down citations to articles that are relevant to your topic.

Author	Title of Article	Source/Periodical Title	Volume, Date, Pages
1			
2			
3			
4			

STEP 6: Disconnect from FirstSearch by typing **BYE**. Once back at the main menu, choose **<P>eriodical Title** and search for each **SOURCE/PERIODICAL TITLE** listed in Step 5.

STEP 7: Write down periodical locations and call numbers. You are now ready to physically retrieve, read, and evaluate the articles.

FIGURE 39-5
FirstSearch Research System

FirstSearch instructions, actions, and commands are always shown on the screen.

Frequently used FirstSearch commands:

F = go **forward** one page or one citation   **H** = access FirstSearch **help** screens

B = go **back** one page or one citation   **S** = begin a new **search**

A = limit search by **adding** new word(s)   **D** = change to another **database**

L = **limit** search by date or category   **BYE** = disconnect and return to
                                                              the local library catalog

FirstSearch Periodical Indexes

General

Database Abbreviation	Database Name and Description
ReadersGuide	*Readers' Guide to Periodical Literature*. Index to articles in **popular magazines**.
NewsAbs	*Newspaper Abstracts*. Index and abstracts to more than 25 U.S. **newspapers.**
PerAbs	*Periodical Abstracts*. Summaries of articles from more than 1,500 **popular and scholarly** periodicals on a wide range of subjects.
Article1st	*Articles First*. Index of articles from nearly 12,500 **journals** on all subjects.

Social Sciences

SocSciInd	*Social Sciences Index*. Index to the literature of all of the social sciences, including **anthropology, economics, geography, criminal justice, political science, and sociology.**
EconLit	*Economic Literature*. Abstracts to research articles in **economics**.
ERIC	*ERIC*. Abstracts to journal articles in the field of **education**.
SocioAbs	*Sociological Abstracts*. Abstracts to articles in all areas of **sociology**.
PAIS Decade	*Public Affairs Information Service*. Abstracts to research on **public policy** issues.

Arts and Humanities

HumanitiesIn	*Humanities Index*. Index to research articles in **history, philosophy, religion, classics, literature, folklore, film studies, performing arts** and related subjects.
ArtIndex	*Art Index*. Index to the major research articles in **painting, sculpture, graphic arts, art history, photography, architecture, interior design**, and related subjects.

Sciences

GenSciIndex	*General Science Index*. Index to the leading **general science** journals.
PsycFIRST	*Psychological Abstracts*. Abstracts from more than 1,300 **psychology** journals.
BasicBIOSIS	*Basic BIOSIS*. Abstracts of research articles in **biology and health**.
ApplSciIndex	*Applied Science Index*. Index to **engineering and technology** research.
INSPEC	*INSPEC*. Abstracts to scientific and technical journals and conference proceedings in **physics, engineering and computer science**.

40. The Bibliography: The Tail That Wags Your Paper

Patricia Gray
Starr Library, Middlebury College, Middlebury, Vermont

Introduction	In comparing the bibliographies of two published works on the same topic, students are expected to use critical thinking to evaluate the choices of research materials made by the authors.
Subject	This exercise has been used in library classes where students are beginning research papers in the social sciences or humanities.
Level of Activity	Undergraduate to graduate
Time Required	Preparation, 15–20 minutes; in class, 15–20 minutes
Size of Class	40 maximum
Preparation	Find bibliographies and copy. Identify what students should notice in the bibliographies.
Class Instructions	Introduce by mentioning that many faculty often look at the bibliography of a research paper before they read the paper. Why? Try to elicit comments about the relationship of a quality bibliography to a quality paper.
Discussion	Use this exercise at the beginning of a library class to push students to think and get involved in the class. The two bibliographies are distributed, and students are asked to work in pairs to analyze and prepare comments for the class in about 5–7 minutes. Do not give the titles of the books or articles from which the bibliographies were taken, and begin discussion by asking students to propose titles.

41. Earned Scholarly Average (ESA): How Can I Tell If It Is a Scholarly Source?

Randall Schroeder
Wartburg College, Waverly, Iowa

Introduction	How reliable is a source as evidence to prove or disprove a thesis? A process of applying a numerical estimate to the reliability is used (Figure 41-1).
Subject	Any
Level of Activity	Undergraduates
Time Required	Preparation, 20 minutes; in class, 50 minutes
Size of Class	20–30
Preparation	Develop a worksheet describing scholarly texts and giving a ranking scale.
Class Instructions	The object of this exercise/game is for students to put together a bibliography with the highest point value, thus avoiding the *Time* and *Redbook* articles that have plagued previous classes.
Discussion	This exercise works in two sessions. In the first, we have the students look for about five or more articles for a project they are currently researching. About a week later we get together to do the ESA. I explain the point values. More important, I also explain what a refereed scholarly journal is and how a student can tell when he or she has found one.
	Obviously there are types of information that elude neat categorization, such as government documents. Also, the values change with different disciplines. Age, for instance, may not be penalized with history or religion research. The important thing, however, is that the students begin to think about what is and is not a reliable source while learning the criteria of scholarly research.

FIGURE 41-1
Earned Scholarly Average
How can I tell if it is a scholarly source?

A warning: This worksheet is a way to help you think about the scholarly worth of a source; that is, how reliable is the source as evidence to prove or disprove a thesis? Most scholars don't use a point system like this to figure out a paper's E.S.A. (earned scholarly average).

Points	Journal or Magazine Article	Book
	Age of source	
3 points	If the article is 1993 or newer	1992 or newer
Subtract 1 point	For each year older than above	
0 points	1990 or older	1989 or older
	Author	
2 points	If the author has written on the topic before	
2 points	If the author is a specialist in the field	
1 point	If the author works for a college or university	
Subtract 1 point	If the author is a journalist	
	Type of source	
3 points	If refereed scholarly journal	
2 points	If scholarly journal	
0 points	If popular magazine (e.g., *Time, Economist*, etc.)	
3 points		Essays in collection
2 points		University press publication
1 point		Each favorable review

Scale

5 points or above = Excellent source, provided it is relevant to your topic
2–4 points = Worth a look
0–1 point = Potentially useful as background material, but keep looking

How do I find out?

Bill Katz / *Magazines for Libraries*
Petersen's Register of Higher Education
Higher Education Directory
Book Review Digest

Check the **bibliography** (back of book, beginning of article, etc.).

Check for a **biography** of the writer.

Check the **title page** and the back of the title page of a journal. If it is published by a college, university or learned society, it is probably a scholarly journal. If it is refereed, it will probably say so.

42. Evaluating Information on the World Wide Web

Ann Scholz-Crane
Rutgers, The State University of New Jersey, Camden, New Jersey

Introduction

The overall goal of this exercise is to have students relate an information need to an actual piece of information and form an opinion about overall quality and relevancy. Students are first given a hypothetical topic statement to read. Next, groups of students are given a URL for a specific document on the WWW and told to evaluate this document based on its quality and its relevancy to the topic statement.

After each group reaches a consensus about whether the document is appropriate, the groups present their conclusions to the class and discuss the process of coming to those conclusions. After completing the exercise, students will be able to:
- identify critical pieces of information within a WWW document that may be used to evaluate its quality;
- determine the overall quality of a WWW document based upon the identified information; and
- determine whether a WWW document is appropriate for a given information need based on its relevancy and quality.

Subject

Any

Level of Activity

Students with some experience searching the WWW

Time Required

Preparation, 2–4 hours; in class, 40 minutes (varies according to how many sources are discussed)

Size of Class

20–30 students working in groups of 3–4

Preparation

1. Write a topic statement (Figure 42-1) and add questions that will stimulate the group's discussion.
2. Select WWW documents and record the URLs to hand out in class. You will want to select more URLs than will actually be used in the class to account for technical difficulties (e.g., bad connections or "moved" site).

3. Make copies of the topic statement, "Evaluating World Wide Web Information" (Figure 42-2), and the "WWW Evaluation Checklist" (Figure 42-3).

Class Instructions

Begin by briefly reviewing the structure of the WWW and making some general comments about the varying levels of quality that exist. Next, introduce the exercise, stating its overall goal and a few key objectives. Hand out the topic statements to the students and ask them to read the statement carefully. Encourage them to circle or make notes of the key points included in the topic statement.

After the students have read the statement, have them break into groups of 3-4, making sure that all members of the group are able to view a computer screen. Explain that you will now be giving each group a URL for a specific document on the WWW that they are to evaluate based on its overall quality and its relevancy to the topic statement they have been given. Inform the class that the WWW Evaluation Checklist will help them with the quality assessment. Questions are included at the bottom of the topic statement to help guide students through key points to address. Inform the class that each group will be expected to report to the class its conclusions and an overview of how that conclusion was reached. Each group should assign a recorder who will make notes.

Evaluation Checklist and the topic statement sheet.

At this point they may want to briefly discuss the topic statement among themselves as you hand out a URL to each group along with the checklist. Once each group has a URL, circulate to be sure that all groups know how to access the address and to answer any questions the students may have. Remind students that they are to evaluate the relevancy and quality of that document only, but they are allowed to explore other documents that may be available at the same site or do quick searches for other relevant documents. You may also need to help students manipulate the URL if all the evaluation criteria are not listed on the document they are given.

Have the class come back together and ask groups to report back to the class. As each group reports, you may wish to display the document so the entire class can relate to the discussion. Ask each group about their assessment of the document's:

• overall quality and reasons behind the decision

- relevancy to the topic and justifications for its inclusion (or omission on a source list for this topic)

Last, ask for any conclusions and additional remarks and questions from other students. If more than one group assessed the same URL, you may want to combine the reports or ask if the other groups agree with the conclusions presented or have anything to add. The instructor may want to conclude with some general remarks to review the main points of the session.

Discussion

A different WWW URL may be given to each group, but for the sake of later discussion it is a good idea to double up the URLs (i.e., two groups evaluate each URL). Students are given a "WWW Evaluation Checklist" to aid in the process of determining the quality of the piece.

It is best to mix the type of documents students are presented and keep the length of the documents selected short. In general, try to include one that is of both high quality and relevancy, one that is high quality but low relevancy, one that is low quality but highly relevant, and one that is both low quality and relevancy. You may also want to simulate the "real world" experience by selecting a few documents where the author or sponsoring institution does not appear on the document itself but may be determined by exploring the larger site.

Students are generally perceptive in catching the subtler points of the exercise, such as tracing an address back to find an author. However, they may need pushing to really evaluate the author and/or the sponsoring institution. You may wish to question the students on the point of author bias. Many times students interpret bias in a negative light. They may need the most help with seeing the relationship between the document and the topic statement. Remind them that there is no pat answer and that they may wish to justify its relevancy based on key points from the topic statement.

This exercise can also lead to a discussion of how this process is similar or dissimilar to evaluating the quality and relevancy of other types of publications.

FIGURE 42-1

EVALUATING WWW INFORMATION

Topic Statement

The Communications Decency Act recently passed the U.S. Congress as a part of the Telecommunications Bill, making it a crime to "initiate the transmission of any comment, request, suggestion, proposal, image or other communication which is lewd, lascivious, filthy, or indecent to minors." This amendment has caused a good deal of controversy over the Internet about who will decide what is fit for children's eyes and whether or not the government or the parents should make these decisions. This resource set explores alternatives to government regulation and censorship, such as commercially available net filtering software and discusses how effective some of these alternatives are. The resources presented are for persons already familiar with the CDA, how to use the Internet, and the types of resources available on the Internet.

Group Discussion Questions

1. What are the key issues in this topic?

2. Do these match issues discussed in your source?
   If so, which ones, and how?

3. Does the level of your source match the intended audience of this topic statement? (explain)

4. Use the "WWW Evaluation Checklist" to determine the overall quality of your source.

5. After assessing the quality of your group's source and how it relates to the topic, would your group recommend the source?
   Justify your decision, listing the key evaluation criteria your group used to reach this conclusion.

Be ready to present the conclusions of your group to the rest of the class

FIGURE 42-2

ESSENTIAL WEB DOCUMENT ELEMENTS

Unlike most print resources such as magazines and journals, which go through a filtering process (i.e., editing, peer review), information on the World Wide Web and the Internet is mostly unfiltered. So using and citing information found on the Web is a little like swimming on a beach without a lifeguard. One of the first things to check a Web document for are its three main elements: header, body, and footer:

[Outline of Web Document]

Within each of these parts, you should be able to assess the following elements:
• author or contact person (usually located in the footer)
• link to local home page (usually located in either the header or footer)
• institution (usually located in header or footer)
• date of creation or revision (usually located in footer)
• Intended audience (determined by examining the body)
• purpose of the information, i.e., does it inform, explain, or persuade? (determined by examining the body)

Find these on each page of promising information and evaluate it based on the "WWW Evaluation Checklist."

FIGURE 42-3
WWW EVALUATION CHECKLIST

AUTHOR
1. Who is the author of the document?
2. Is the author the original creator of the information?
    ❏ Yes   ❏ No   ❏ Can't tell
3. Does he or she list his or her occupation, years of experience, position, or education? If so, list here:

4. With this information or lack of it, do you feel this person is qualified to write on the topic?
    ❏ Yes   ❏ No If yes, why?

LOCAL INSTITUTION OR HOME PAGE
5. What institution (company, government, university, etc.) or Internet provider supports this information?
6. If it is a commercial Internet provider, does the author appear to have any affiliation with a larger institution?
    ❏ Yes   ❏ No
7. If it is an institution, is it a national one?
    ❏ Yes   ❏ No
8. Does the institution appear to filter the information appearing under its name?
    ❏ Yes   ❏ No
9. Does the author's affiliation with this particular institution appear to bias the information?
    ❏ Yes   ❏ No

DOCUMENT INFORMATION
10. When was the information created or last updated?
11. What appears to be the purpose for this information? (explain)
    ❏ Inform   ❏ Explain   ❏ Persuade

CONCLUSION
12. Given all the information you determined from above, is this document appropriate for your topic?
    ❏ Yes   ❏ No
    If yes, explain why, including any reservations you might have.

Parts of this checklist were adapted from Judith Pask, Roberta Kramer, and Scott Mandernack, *The Savvy Student's Guide to Library Research*. West Lafayette, Ind.: John W. Hicks Undergraduate Library, 1993.

43. Evaluating Internet Sources

Karen Paul Topham
Brookdale Community College, Lincroft, New Jersey

Introduction	This exercise is one part of a larger course called Computers in Libraries, which stresses evaluation of tools and sources. This assignment works well once group cohesiveness has been established. If trust has been built in class, students are less afraid of searching in the presence of other students and of criticism regarding the sites found.
Subject	Can be used in any area where Internet sources will be used.
Level of Activity	Any. Students should have some familiarity with computers, and prior Internet searching experience is recommended.
Time Required	30 minutes
Size of Class	12-16 students
Preparation	Collect a number of newspaper articles discussing one particular Internet site or topical sites. Watch out for "dead" sites!
Class Instructions	Divide the class into groups of 3–4. Within each group, 1–2 students will take notes, and 2 students will describe the site. After 10 minutes, students' roles are switched. The students are to evaluate the sites for format, content, ease of use, reliability, relevancy, and usefulness. Each group then presents its findings to the class.
Discussion	A good final question might be, "Would you bookmark this site on the workstation at the reference desk?" The inference is that if it's bookmarked, it will be a heavily used and/or a site of very valuable information.

44. Using the Online Catalog

Donna J. Davidoff and Albert F. Riess
E. H. Butler Library, Buffalo State College, State University of New York,
Buffalo, New York

Introduction

The goal of this exercise is to promote a student's ability to make effective use of the online catalog. Students evaluate the appropriateness of citations for a particular research need.

Subject

Any

Level of Activity

Any

Time Required

10–15 minutes to explain the activity and for students to review printouts; 20 minutes for class discussion

Size of Class

25–35 students (Adaptable for a smaller class)

Preparation

Gather together the necessary printouts. Adapt the worksheets shown in Figure 44-1 for your library and copy two of each. Search your online catalog and create a printout of about 30 items on teenage pregnancy, making sure that some of the items are appropriate for each of the worksheet topics.

Class Instructions

1. Divide the class into groups of two.
2. Each team receives the same printout from the online catalog of about 30 items on the topic of teenage pregnancy.
3. Each team is given a worksheet placing them in a certain scenario. They are asked to choose the items from the printout which would best meet their information needs.

Discussion

In class, students discuss and explain, in general, how they usually review online catalog printouts to select what materials to use: title, date of publication, familiar author, accessibility, etc. Teams then discuss their specific choices for this assignment with feedback from other members of the class, some of whom may have the same scenario. Attention is directed to more subtle hints found in citations: subtitles, subject headings, presence of an index or bibliography, publisher, call number location, etc.

FIGURE 44-1

Name:_____

Class:_____

ONLINE CATALOG IN-CLASS ASSIGNMENT

> You are a social worker major starting an internship with a local social services agency that works with pregnant teenagers and their families.

1. Review the books on your printout and choose those which would best meet your specific needs. Be prepared to explain your choices. List the numbers of the books you chose below:

2. What would you do to find more books on this topic for your particular needs?

FIGURE 44–1 cont.

Name:_____

Class:_____

ONLINE CATALOG IN-CLASS ASSIGNMENT

> You are a junior high school teacher who would like to prepare a lesson plan for your classes on teenage pregnancy.

1. Review the books on your printout and choose those which would best meet your specific needs. Be prepared to explain your choices. List the numbers of the books you chose below:

2. What would you do to find more books on this topic for your particular needs?

FIGURE 44-1 cont.

Name: _____

Class: _____

ONLINE CATALOG IN-CLASS ASSIGNMENT

> You are an actor who just landed the lead in a broadway play which chronicles the day-to-day activities and thoughts of a pregnant teenager.
> You play the teenager.

1. Review the books on your printout and choose those which would best meet your specific needs. Be prepared to explain your choices. List the numbers of the books you chose below:

2. What would you do to find more books on this topic for your particular needs?

FIGURE 44-1

Name: _____

Class: _____

ONLINE CATALOG IN-CLASS ASSIGNMENT

> You are the parent of a teenager who has just announced at the dinner table that she is pregnant.

1. Review the books on your printout and choose those which would best meet your specific needs. Be prepared to explain your choices. List the numbers of the books you chose below:

2. What would you do to find more books on this topic for your particular needs?

FIGURE 44-1

Name: _____

Class: _____

ONLINE CATALOG IN-CLASS ASSIGNMENT

> You are a staff member of an urban government agency and you want to research the growing problem of teenage pregnancy and set up some policies and programs to help deal with it.

1. Review the books on your printout and choose those which would best meet your specific needs. Be prepared to explain your choices. List the numbers of the books you chose below:

2. What would you do to find more books on this topic for your particular needs?

45. Selecting Appropriate Journal Articles

Gail Gradowski
Santa Clara University, Santa Clara, California

Introduction

Do you wish there were a way to teach freshmen a strategy other than "pick the first 5, any 5" for selecting periodical articles? Would you like to ban the use of *Time* and *Newsweek* in freshman papers? This exercise is for you! It attempts to broaden student horizons in the periodical arena by introducing them to different types of periodicals and their distinguishing characteristics.

Subject

Freshman writing

Level of Activity

Basic

Time Required

Preparation, 10 minutes if all materials are present (20 minutes to pull the journals); in class, 65 minutes

Size of Class

24 students (Best if done in 8 groups of 2–3)

Preparation

Number the tables where students will sit from 1 to 8. At each table put one "From Different Perspectives" worksheet (Figure 45-1), one "Summary" sheet (Figure 45-2), three copies of the handout "Types of Periodicals" (Figure 45-3), and two periodicals containing articles from the citation list in Figure 45-1.

Class Instructions

1. As students enter the room, give them a number 1–8 for seating assignments. Make some brief introductory comments on the goal and procedures of the session (see above). Ask some opening questions/statements, such as:

    "Name some periodicals."
    "If I gave you 5 minutes, how many do you think you could name?"

2. It is often interesting to ask: "How many periodicals do you think this library subscribes to?" In longer classes, it is sometimes useful to follow up on some of their answers:

    "You seem mostly familiar with popular periodicals; what is another type of periodical?"
    "Can you give me an example?"

"What makes it different? How can you tell?"
"What is the value in using different types?"
"Why not just use *Time* or *Newsweek*?"

3. Go over the first TWO tasks from the worksheet, paraphrasing the worksheet. A volume of *Isis* (v. 83) is kept in the room for this purpose.

4. Ask them how long it will take them to do the worksheet for their PAIR. Emphasize that they must do two. Set the timer accordingly. You may need to adjust later, but generally they will finish in 10–15 minutes.

5. Go over the next two questions. Make sure they see the list, "Articles Used by All Groups." Again, give an example (the article on pp. 61–79 of *Isis* works well), making clear that question 3 does not require a detailed content analysis of the article.

6. Again, ask how long they think they will need. These two questions generally take less time.

7. Tell them they have 5 minutes to put the information they have gathered into a very short and sweet and informative SUMMARY for the rest of the class.

8. Get their attention and begin calling on groups to give their presentations. Emphasize that they have not a second more than 2 minutes. Do not question their conclusions too much. Accept anything that makes any sense and indicates that they are looking at things reasonably. Some of the "periodical type" distinctions are quite fuzzy. If they are way off, however, do question their conclusions.

9. As they go around, jot down on the board in very general terms, the "authorities" that are mentioned.

After all the groups are done, give them a minute to survey the list of authorities and ask, "What would we want to add?" and, then, "Where would we look?" Included in this VERY BRIEF class discussion would be the question of where/how all of the material used in this class was found: *Expanded Academic Index*, bibliography on animal rights, *Philosopher's Index, Education Index, Biological and Agricultural Index, Religion Index*. This would logically be extended into how one would go about finding whatever it was they suggested adding.

FIGURE 45-1
From Different Perspectives; *or,* **What's your Angle?**

Choosing your information sources should involve a strategy more complex than **Pick One, Any One**! So, in this exercise, you will be examining periodical articles on the topic of **ANIMAL RIGHTS.** They have been selected for the **variety** they represent.

As a group you will be examining a pair of periodicals, each periodical as a whole as well as a specific article within it.

Reflect, scrutinize, and discuss these periodicals, using *Types of Periodicals* as a guide. Then, provide thoughtful, insightful, and brief answers to the questions below.

For the first two questions, examine one *entire issue* **of each periodical. Look especially at the feature articles.**

A. Succinctly *(no wasted words)* describe each of the periodicals you have. Include in your description the intended audience *(this could be the academic discipline, profession, etc.),* the credentials *(or background or authority)* of the author**s** *(remember, you are looking at all of them for this question, not just one)* in general terms *(for example, journalists, biologists, Jesuits),* the sponsor *(this may be the publisher)* of the journal.

B. Using what you decided in A., describe the **types** of periodical you have. Use the categories from the handout, *Types of Periodicals,* for your description. In each case, you have **two different** types.

Now look at the cited articles. Find yours on the list "Articles Used by All Groups" on the back of this worksheet.
• Consider what type of article each is *(news, editorial, analysis, investigative report, report of research, etc.).* Keep in mind that every article in a particular journal is not necessarily the same *type* of article.

• What is the background/credentials of each of the articles' authors?

• Finally, prepare a summary of your answers to the questions above for the class.

You will have no more than two minutes to give this presentation!

FIGURE 45-1 cont.
Articles Used by All Groups

"An introduction to the philosophical presuppositions of the animal liberation/rights movement." Richard P.Vance. *JAMA*, October 7, 1992 v268 p1715 (5).

Clifton, Merritt.. "Fur farms: where the sun doesn't shine." *ANIMALS AGENDA* 11(9):12–15 November 1991

"Why worry about the animals?" Jean Bethke Elshtain. *The Progressive*, March 1990 v54 n3 p17(5).

"Difficult deicisions: animal rights." Jal S. Parakh and Irwin L. Slesnik.. *The Science Teacher*, April 1989 v56 n3 p234–5.

"Blacks? Animals? Homosexuals? What is a minority?" (W. B. Allen address) (transcript) *Vital Speeches*, Jan 15, 1990 v56 n7 p204 (4).

"Animals rights versus humanism – the charge of speciesism." K. Shapiro. *Journal of Humanistic Psychology*, Spring 1990 v30 n2 p.9 (29).

"Animal rights and feminist theory." Josephine Donovan. *Signs*, Wntr 1990 v15 n2 p350 (26).

"Fur flies in pelt dispute." Michael Kantor. *Sierra*, July-Aug, 1988 v73 n4 p26 (3).

"An uncaged vision of nonhuman creation." (Editorial) James M. Wall. *Christian Century*, October 25, 1989 v106 n31 p947(2).

> Author: Linzey, Andrew
> Title: "Liberation Theology and the Oppression of Animals"
> Journal: *Scottish Journal of Theology* 46 no. 4, 507–525 1993

"Creature teachers." (unbalanced emphasis on animal rights) (Column) Matthew Scully. *National Review*, May 10, 1993 v45 n9 p.56 (3).

> Author: Rowan, Andrew N.; Rollin, Bernard E.
> Title: "Animal research—for and against: a philosophical, social, and historical
>   perspective."
> Source: *Perspectives in Biology and Medicine* v. 27 (Autumn '83) p.1–17 bibl.

"On the rights of an ape." (Column) Daniel W. McShea. *Discover*, Feb 1994 v15 n2 p34 (4).

"Take me, take my guinea pigs." (animal rights and laboratory rodents) Gail Vines. *New Scientist*, Jan 21, 1995 v145 n1961 p49(2).

"Everyday morality and animal rights." Steve Sapontzis. *Between the Species*, Summer 1987 v3 p107 (21).

FIGURE 45–1 cont.

Sapontzis, Steve F. "Animal Rights and Biomedical Research." *Journal of Value Inquiry*, 26 (1), 73–86, Ja 92.

"Animal rights: an evolutionary perspective." Kenneth L. Feder. *The Humanist*, July August 1990 v50 p5 (3).

Author: Morrison, Adrian R.
Title: What's wrong with 'animal rights'
Source: *The American School Board Journal* v. 179 (Jan. '92) p.20–23.

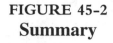

FIGURE 45-2
Summary

For further discussion. . .

Consider the two articles you have. Consider the topic of animal rights *(or a relevant subtopic suggested by the two articles)*. Consider the two perspectives represented by the two articles. Now, think about what other perspectives would be relevant to the issue. Suggest another perspective you could logically seek that would add to your research on this issue. Tell us how you would go about looking for such an item. For more details on any aspect, consult with a librarian or your instructor!

FIGURE 45-3
TYPES OF PERIODICALS

For more details on any aspect, consult with a librarian or your instructor!

	SCHOLARLY & RESEARCH JOURNALS	PROFESSIONAL, TRADE & INDUSTRY JOURNALS	JOURNALS OF COMMENTARY	NEWSPAPERS & OPINION	POPULAR MAGAZINES
Examples	Sociological Review New England Journal of Medicine Bioscience American Quarterly	RN Automotive News Library Journal Restaurants & Institutions	National Review Mother Jones In These Times America	New York Times Washington Post Wall Street Journal San Jose Mercury News	Time Newsweek U.S. News & World Report Sports Illustrated
Value & Uses	Reports of original research, theoretical, experimental or applied. In-depth analysis of topics. Lengthy articles. Substantial book reviews. Many are refereed/peer reviewed.	Current trends, news & events in a particular field. Product, company and biographical information. Statistics, including forecasts. Some book reviews.	Commentary on political & social issues. Often source of specific political viewpoint, e.g., conservative, liberal, or specific interest group. Speeches & interviews (excerpts, usually) Often substantial book reviews	Current information News stories Local & regional focus Analysis & opinion on current events, Speeches Some book reviews	Current events & news. Primary source for popular culture Short articles Interviews Some book reviews
Language	College-educated; uses the technical vocabulary of the discipline.	Written for practitioners so uses jargon of the field	Written for a general, educated audience	Written for a general, educated audience	Non-technical, often simple language
Authors	Researchers, academics, scholars, and such.	Practitioners or journalists with subject expertise	Often display the greatest variety of authors, some writers, some specialists, sometimes members of the sponsoring organization	Journalists	Journalists
Sources	Footnotes & bibliographies; documentation often very extensive.	Sources often cited, but full documentation is not always provided	Highly variable; sources often cited but full documentation is not always provided.	Sources are rarely cited in full	Original sources can be obscure.
Publishers	Professional organizations, universities, research institutes & scholarly presses.	Commercial/trade publishers or professional associations.	Commercial/trade publisher or nonprofit organizations	Commercial/trade publisher	Commercial/trade publisher.
Graphics	Graphs, charts & tables. Ads are very rare.	Charts, tables, illustrations Ads related to the profession/industry	Varies a lot; some have graphics, color and ads	Pictures & charts Some ads	Glitzy; many graphics and pictures. Lots of color ads
Access Tools	Expanded Academic Index and specialized indexes such as: Sociological Abstracts, PsycLIT, Communication Abstracts.	ABI-Inform, Business Periodicals Index, Predicasts F & S Index & some specialized indexes, like PsycLIT and Compendex	Expanded Academic Index, PAIS, Alternative Press Index	National Newspaper Index & indexes to specific newspapers: San Jose Mercury News New York Times Times (London)	Readers Guide. Expanded Academic Index also covers a few of the newsier ones.

46. Turning Instruction Upside Down: Evaluation and Database Search Skills

Paula R. Dempsey
DePaul University Library, Chicago, Illinois

Introduction

This exercise reverses the order of the search process to emphasize the evaluation of citations found in bibliographic databases. It is a practical application of evaluation skills that prepares students to use intermediate search sets to refine a search. It can be used as a separate module or as the core of a longer session on organization of library materials and research methods.

Subject

Any

Level of Activity

Undergraduate to graduate

Time Required

Preparation, 20 minutes; in class, 20 minutes

Size of Class

Up to 40

Preparation

1. Develop a sample research question appropriate to the class content (e.g., **How does advertising attempt to teach children to influence their parents' buying decisions?**) and design a basic search statement of two terms (e.g., **children and advertising**).
2. Run the search statement on four or five appropriate databases, and print out the first five records from each search *without evaluating them.* Cut the printouts into individual records—there should be at least one for each student in the class. (Step 2 can be done by a student assistant.)

Discussion/ Class Instruction

Introduce your sample research question, preferably as part of a discussion of ways to develop a research topic.

Distribute one record to each student and explain the search statement that was used to pull them up. Stress that the first five records only were printed out, regardless of content. Ask students to circle the search terms wherever they appear in the record. Explain the terms *record* and *field* and note that the terms can appear in any field in the record. Have one student read the field labels in his or her record. Ask whether anyone has different fields.

Give students 2–3 minutes to work in small groups to do the following:
• Discuss the records your group has, and decide which is the **best** one to start with for our research question.
• List the fields you used to make your decision.
• Be ready to explain how the other fields could be used to make this decision.

Go around to each table during the discussion to clarify the directions and answer questions. After 2–3 minutes, have one person in each group read the title of their "best" article and explain which fields they used to make the decision.

The following fields will probably be mentioned. At the end, explain the usefulness of any that do not emerge from the discussion: Subject (Relevance); Title (Relevance, Difficulty level); Date (Currency); Length (Is the article too short to bother with? Longer than you care to read?); Source (Scholarly, popular?); and Authors (Affiliation).

Another significant criterion for students is, "Can I get this in time?" This makes a good transition to an explanation of procedures for locating the full text of articles: which periodicals does the institution own, ILL requests, etc. You can use some of the "best" articles to demonstrate the process.

If the exercise is used as part of a longer session, do it before a demonstration of searching databases. You can draw on the skills from this exercise to help students refine their searches using intermediate search sets. For example, have them select the best search terms from the "best" articles to begin a live database demonstration, then narrow the search using more specific terms.

Section V

Discipline-Oriented Instruction

Edited by Gail Gradowski

The exercises in this section demonstrate some ways in which library instruction can be focused on a particular academic discipline. They include a sampling from the humanities, social sciences and sciences, that demonstrate a wide range of types of activities that can serve as excellent models adaptable to any discipline.

The first exercise, "Flow of Information for Art Students," is a short mini-exercise that gets students thinking about the generation and, therefore, the retrieval of information about art and artists.

"Business Resources" focuses on selected business periodicals. It is an excellent example of a highly unstructured exercise that is entirely student-focused; therefore, it is definitely not for someone just trying out active learning for the first time!

"Authors and Criticism" and "Marketing Management" are structured similarly, falling into a general type often termed fetch-and-report. They do, though, two very different variations on that format. "Marketing Management" is much more tightly structured, heavily orches-trated, and uses a wider variety of tools and resources. "Authors and Criticism" uses the fetch-and-report format just for the exploration of reference books. Either would serve as an excellent model for someone wanting to try out this technique.

"Library Research in the Sciences" sounds general but, in fact, is very much a critical think-ing exercise that guides students through the intellectual process of translating a topical need into the vocabulary and structure of different databases. And it's not just relevant for science, either!

"Computer Science Library Resource Challenge" and "Desperately Seeking Communica-tion Information" both use teams and a series of highly structured exercises to get students to explore a variety of tools and techniques related to their disciplines.

"Introducing Women's Studies Resources" is a nice ending to this chapter as it incorporates a number of techniques used in other exercises in this chapter and deals with periodicals, indexes and reference books in this interdisciplinary field.

47. Flow of Information Exercise for Art Students

Monica Fusich
Willis Library, University of North Texas, Denton, Texas

Introduction

I use this exercise in classes in which students need to research a contemporary artist. The objective of this exercise is to facilitate critical thinking about the flow of information in the art world, enabling students to understand the challenges of locating information on contemporary artists. Since it is used at the beginning of class, it also serves as an icebreaker.

Subject

Art

Level of Activity

Basic or intermediate

Time Required

10 minutes

Size of Class

10–25 students

Preparation

Prepare an overhead showing a grid with three headings (or write them on the board):
- Type of information
- Time
- Access

Class Instructions

Ask a volunteer to tell the class what type of artist he or she is. The volunteer answers, for example, "printmaker." Ask the class to brainstorm on where they would expect to find information about the printmaker. Typical answers include: gallery flyers, word of mouth, radio announcements, article in the student paper, and article in the local paper. Put their ideas on the board in the "Type of Information" column.

Imagine that it is five years from now, and your classmate has become a famous artist. What other places would you look for more information? Typical responses include national newspapers and art magazines. Prompt them to list other sources, such as books, exhibition catalogs, art encyclopedias, and biographical directories and add these ideas to the board.

Ask them to estimate how quickly information is disseminated in these various formats (e.g., word of mouth—immediately). Add this information to the "Time" column.

Ask the class how they would expect to access the various forms of information. This leads into a brief overview of indexes, catalogs, and special artist finding tools.

Discussion

I do this exercise at the beginning of class and it immediately grabs their attention, because they like the idea of one of them making it big as an artist. It also helps establish a rapport with the class and makes them feel more comfortable interacting and asking questions. It also teaches them what types of information are available and how to access them for their assignment.

48. Business Resources

Margaret Fain and Jeri Traw
Kimbel Library, Coastal Carolina University, Myrtle Beach, South Carolina

Introduction	The objectives of the class are to introduce entering business majors to the primary magazines, journals, and newspapers in the field and introduce them to the types of resources available for doing business research. This is designed as a very basic introduction to resources and librarians. The structure of the exercise demands that students come up with the resources. The librarian only mentions resources that students have not listed.
Subject	Business
Level of Activity	Undergraduate
Time Required	Preparation, about 30 minutes; in class, total class time
Size of Class	15 to 50
Preparation	Pull copies of popular business magazines, newspapers, and journals. Develop a list of business resources that students could use in future projects and reports.
Class Instructions	Ask students to list three business magazines, two business journals, and one business newspaper. Ask pairs of students to compare their lists and have them list the sources on the board. List all the sources the students suggest on the board and show samples from the copies brought to class. Provide supportive feedback for their choices. Then ask student pairs to list all the sources they can think of that might be useful in a business paper or project from their area of concentration. Again, list these responses on the board. When all pairs have responded, ask leading questions to elicit additional resources that they have missed.

Discussion

1. Be supportive of all answers. Give credit for news magazines and general newspapers, point out strengths of all sources listed.
2. There are no wrong answers in this exercise.
3. Call on pairs to start with and then ask for and expect them to volunteer.
4. Pairs with no answers should be asked to come up with one while you ask another group.
5. For larger classes, groups of three or four can be used.

49. Authors and Criticism: Exploring Sources While Learning About the Library

Corinne Ebbs
Westfield State College, Westfield, Massachusetts

Introduction

This exercise is designed to help students find information about authors and literary criticism. The class begins with brainstorming about the types of sources students would expect to use for a literary research project. The librarian records their ideas on large sheets of paper, transparencies, or chalkboards and asks students where they would expect to find these resources in the library.

Basic information about the OPAC is covered, and then students are divided into groups and sent out into the library to locate and review three relevant sources. They may choose any author or time period, but each source must be of a different type, and at least one must be a reference source. Remind students that the criteria they use to evaluate print works should apply to electronic sources as well. It is helpful to circulate when students are reviewing their materials to answer any questions about the exercises or about the materials themselves. After 15 minutes, the students return to class, and each group reports its findings.

There may not be time for very large classes to report back, but their evaluations can be solicited in writing. Written evaluations should include the title and author of the materials being reviewed.

A second class to evaluate electronic sources with this method may be desirable. By comparing information gained from networked indexes and the Internet to the information they were able to retrieve from printed materials, students can begin to form a basis from which to conduct research more realistically and more meaningfully.

Subject

Literary research

Level of Activity

Upper-division or graduate students

Time Required

1½–2 hours

Size of Class	10–20 students

Preparation

1. Select 3–4 different authors from the time period or area in question.
2. Make sure these authors are well covered in different types of sources in your collection.
3. Prepare a list of types of sources to which students can refer (e.g., bibliography, dictionary, index, handbook, book of criticism).
4. Alert the reference librarians on duty during your class.

Discussion

Brainstorm with the class. Feel free to give hints if there are no takers, but remember to WAIT for responses before jumping in!

• What types of sources would you use to find out about an author? Why?
• What types of sources would you use to find criticism? How would each source be useful?
• In what types of sources would you look for criticism?
• How are these types different from one another?

Write down contributions so that the class can see them and you can refer to them later. Ask the class to tell you where in the library you might find these sources (sounds obvious, but even grad students need this).

Review the OPAC—do this even if this is an upper-level class. Illustrate the difference between subject and keyword searching. Point out oft-forgotten or neglected commands. (If you work reference, you will know what these are for your particular system.) Remind students how to locate videos, journals (especially if there is not a separate index in your system for journal titles!), special collection items, etc. Point out information necessary to locate the materials in your library.

If class time is short, mention relevant indexes available for locating journal articles, but refrain from covering them in class. The list of evaluative questions can be modified for shorter student reports in larger classes, although getting part of the way through the full list of questions may encourage some students to experiment further with evaluation.

When the students head out to do the assignment, go with them to the reference area and circulate so that the normal flow of reference doesn't get disturbed by your students' queries.

Class Instructions

1. Your group must locate three (3) library items that meet the following criteria:
   - They all must have information on _____.
   - Your author's name cannot be included in the titles of any materials you bring back to class.
   - Each source must be a different type of source. (It is wise to spend a minute re-connecting this to the earlier brainstorming.)
   - At least one source must come from the reference area.

2. In 15 minutes, return to the classroom with your three items. Be prepared to describe them to your classmates using these Description Guidelines:

   - What type of source is it?
   - How will it be helpful to you (e.g., what type of information is available from it, does it refer you to other sources, is it a primary or secondary source)?
   - Where in the library did you find it?
   - When was it published? Will this date influence your use of this material? Why or why not?
   - Where was this published/created (what country)?
   - Who is responsible for this work? Is there any information available on his/her/their affiliation(s) that might lead you to believe he/she/they were experts in the field?
   - What information does the foreword and/or introduction give?
   - For whom was this material intended (level of education, interest, etc.)?
   - What was the purpose of this work? (Is it an overview, a review, exhaustive, etc.?)
   - If there is an index, describe it. What does it index? Experiment with references—are page numbers accurate?
   - Does the information you retrieve make sense to you?
   - How easy is this source to use?
   - If the material you retrieved is not in print format (e.g., a video, CD-ROM) or is a journal or periodical, what can you tell us about it?

50. Marketing Management

Elizabeth Lukacs
Le Moyne College, Syracuse, New York

Introduction

This three-hour session was designed to overcome the problems associated with teaching groups of MBA students who come to class tired and hungry after working all day. Students work in pre-existing teams which removes some pressure and makes the session more enjoyable. Each team reviews three titles from a list of resources they will be using throughout the semester. They make brief presentations to the class, the most successful being those that clearly demonstrate how the newfound information may be applied to their case studies. Most of these reports encourage more questions and rapid note-taking than when the librarian is the only presenter. The student presentations will be quite good despite the short time (15 minutes) allotted for review and analysis. The instructor and the librarian share responsibility for moving students at appropriate times, helping students locate resources and assisting them in using the resources and even finding applications for their cases.

Subject

Marketing

Level of Activity

Introduction to secondary sources in marketing for graduate students

Time Required

3 hours

Size of Class

30 students

Preparation

1. (First time only) Customize call numbers on the *Company & Industry Data* bibliography (Figure 50-1) for your own library.
2. Photocopy one agenda for each student (Figure 50-2).
3. Photocopy one *Company & Industry Data* bibliography for each student.
4. Assign each group three titles from the *Company & Industry Data* bibliography (Figures 50-3 and 50-4).
5. Prepare one card for each group that lists the three titles (Figure 50-5).
6. Photocopy one Reference Tool Evaluation Worksheet (Figure 50-6) for each group.
7. Prepare one transparency of the Report on the Tobacco Industry (Figure 50-7).

Class Instructions

The purpose of this session is to introduce the marketing resources you will need to complete your case studies this semester. We will begin by learning how to search our online catalog and one or two business-related periodical indexes. Then we will review the Company and Industry Data bibliography that corresponds to the card your team was given when you arrived. I will demonstrate how to analyze and present your assigned titles and then we will move to the reference area where each team will review three titles. After 45 minutes we will meet back in the classroom and each team will report its findings. After reports, we will take a break followed by a demonstration of LEXIS®/NEXIS®.

Discussion

1. Ask students to sit at tables with their team members. At the start of the session, give each team a card with three numbers (Figure 50-5); each number corresponds to a title on the Company & Industry Data bibliography (Figure 50-1).

2. Make a brief presentation on competitive intelligence and information literacy that concludes with students critiquing a brief but problematic bibliography, Report on the Tobacco Industry (Figure 50-7). The success that they are able to demonstrate in this exercise gives them some confidence to tackle the more complex activities ahead.

3. Review the *Standard Industrial Classification Manual* for students in the same way that they will be expected to present their assigned titles to the group. The review covers the book's purpose, arrangement, content, and how it is used to find information related to a case study.

4. Students leave the classroom. They have 45 minutes to review their titles. Each team reviews the first title on its card during the first 15 minutes, the second title during the second 15 minutes, and the third title in the final 15 minutes. Coordinate teams so that they do not compete for the same title at the same time.

5. After the class returns to the classroom, call on each group in the order of their assigned titles (Figures 50-3 and 50-4). Both the instructor and the librarian make comments when students do not mention significant features or possible applications of the titles they are presenting.

FIGURE 50-1
Sample Bibliography (Preparation steps 1 and 3)

COMPANY AND INDUSTRY DATA

Guides to Information   **Location**

1. BUSINESS INFORMATION SOURCES

2. BUSINESS RANKINGS ANNUAL

3. ENCYCLOPEDIA OF BUSINESS INFORMATION SOURCES

4. INTERNATIONAL BUSINESS INFORMATION

5. STATISTICAL ABSTRACT OF THE UNITED STATES

Company Information   **Location**

6. FINANCE, INSURANCE & REAL ESTATE USA

7. HOOVER'S GUIDE TO PRIVATE COMPANIES

8. HOOVER'S HANDBOOK OF WORLD BUSINESS

9. INTERNATIONAL DIRECTORY OF COMPANY
HISTORIES. VOL. 1–13

10. MANUFACTURING USA

11. MILLION DOLLAR DIRECTORY. VOL. 1–6

12. SERVICE INDUSTRIES USA

13. STANDARD & POOR'S CORPORATION RECORDS.
VOL. A–Z and DAILY NEWS (looseleaf, continuous revision) VOL. 1–8

14. STANDARD & POOR'S REGISTER OF CORPORATIONS,
DIRECTORS AND EXECUTIVES.VOL. 1-3 and Suppl.

15. STANDARD & POOR'S INDUSTRY SURVEYS (quarterly)

FIGURE 50-1 Cont.

16. VALUE LINE INVESTMENT SURVEY (weekly)

17. WHOLESALE AND RETAIL TRADE USA

Company Information Online   **Location**

18. COMPUSTAT

19. GALE BUSINESS RESOURCES

20. INVESTEXT

21. MOODY'S COMPANY DATA

22. MOODY'S INTERNATIONAL COMPANY DATA

23. NATIONAL TRADE DATA BANK

Indexes   **Location**

24. PREDICASTS F&S INDEX U.S. (weekly)

25. PREDICASTS BASEBOOK (annual)

Indexes Online   **Location**

26. BUSINESS PERIODICALS INDEX ONDISC

27. FIRSTSEARCH databases (selective list):
    BUSINESS DATELINE
    GPO
    PAIS DECADE
    WORLDSCOPE

28. NEWSPAPER ABSTRACTS ON DISK

FIGURE 50-2
Sample Agenda (Preparation step 2)

MARKETING MANAGEMENT

The class will meet in _____. Please sit at the same table with your case study teammates.

The purpose of this class is to introduce the major research tools used in finding company and industry information. You will work in teams to research the company previously assigned in class. The session is structured as follows:

6:00–6:05	Introduction
6:05–6:25	Demonstrations of: • library's online catalog • Business Periodicals Ondisc • FirstSearch: GPO database
6:25–6:35	Review of Company and Industry Data bibliography. Demonstration of how to analyze information in a research tool and present findings to the class. Assignment of titles on the bibliography to be analyzed.
6:35–7:20	Go to the library's reference area and review the assigned titles (title 1 in the first 15 minutes, title 2 in the second 15 minutes, title 3 in the last 15 minutes). Your instructors will be in the area to assist you.
7:20–8:00	Return to _____. Teams will report their findings to the rest of the class.
8:00–8:10	BREAK Sign-up for one-hour hands-on LEXIS®/NEXIS® training session.
8:10–9:00	Introduction to LEXIS®/NEXIS®. Demonstration of L/N.

FIGURE 50–3
Title Review Plan (Preparation step 4)

Instructor prepares a plan insuring that all titles are reviewed, that certain types of resources are assigned to each group, and that groups do not compete for workstations or print sources at the same time.

1st 15 min.	Group 1 Title 6&7	Group 2 Title 7&8	Group 3 Title 1	Group 4 Title 22	Group 5 Title 3
	Group 6 Title 4	Group 7 Title 5	Group 8 Title 13&14	Group 9 Title 28	Group 10 Title 18
2nd 15 min.	Group 1 Title 19	Group 2 Title 4	Group 3 Title 13&14	Group 4 Title 15&16	Group 5 Title 22
	Group 6 Title 24	Group 7 Title 23	Group 8 Title 3	Group 9 Title 2	Group 10 Title 1
3rd 15 min.	Group 1 Title 5	Group 2 Title 20	Group 3 Title 21	Group 4 Title 2	Group 5 Title 25
	Group 6 Title 26	Group 7 Title 15&16	Group 8 Title 9	Group 9 Title 11	Group 10 Title 12&17

FIGURE 50-4
Title Report Plan (Preparation step 4)

Groups report on the titles they reviewed. The instructor works through the bibliography, title by title, and calls on predetermined groups to provide the reports.

TITLE	GROUP	TITLE	GROUP
1.	10	15. & 16.	4
2.	9	18.	10
3.	5	19.	1
4.	6	20.	2
5.	7	21.	3
6. & 10.	1	22.	4
7. & 8.	2	23.	7
9.	8	24.	6
11.	9	25.	5
12. & 17.	10	26.	6
13. & 14.	3	27.	8
		28.	9

FIGURE 50-5
Group Title Card (Preparation step 5)

A card is distributed to each group at the beginning of class.

Group 5

COMPANY AND INDUSTRY DATA bibliography titles to be reviewed:

Title 3
Title 22
Title 25

Please return this card at the end of class. Thank you.

FIGURE 50-6
Reference Tool Evaluation Worksheet (Preparation step 6)

Make note of the title and number of volumes or parts. Notice how the source is arranged. Does it have information you can use for your project? Describe not only what you found out about your company and industry but also how you found it. Describe any special feature or some aspect of the title you found interesting. Did you find the source difficult or easy to use?

Title 1:

Title 2:

Title 3:

FIGURE 50-7
Sample Bibliography for In-Class Critique (Preparation step 7)

REPORT ON THE TOBACCO INDUSTRY

Bibliography

THE ECONOMIC IMPACT OF CIGARETTE SMOKING ON THE AMERICAN HEALTHCARE SYSTEM, A RESEARCH REPORT. Issued jointly by the American Tobacco Producers and the Tobacco Research Council. 1995.

Smith, Steve. "Sold American! Exporting the smoking habit to Japan." *READER'S DIGEST*, January 1996, pp. 23–25.

"The state of the tobacco industry: an annual report." *JOURNAL OF AMERICAN AGRICULTURE*, May 1967, pp. 14–28.

51. Library Research in the Sciences

Jeanne Davidson
Oregon State University, Corvallis, Oregon

Introduction

This is a single-session class used with first-year honors writing students who have already received a general library tour. It was designed to introduce students to library research in the sciences with particular emphasis on choosing appropriate databases and developing search strategies. Students work in small groups to determine answers to set questions and report their results to the rest of the class.

Objectives of the class were to:
• Introduce students to the nature of the research process, including defining the topic, identifying sources, locating sources and evaluating the results as part of a circular process.
• Have students begin to critically evaluate finding aids, such as indexes, as well as the actual sources of information.

Subject

Sciences (Could be modified to fit any topic in which choice of database, search strategy and evaluation are necessary for success.)

Level of Activity

Basic

Time Required

Preparation, 30–60 minutes (1 to 2 hours the first time); in-class, 60–90 minutes

Size of Class

25, divided into 4–5 small groups

Preparation

1. Survey students in advance about their topics and any other concerns for research they may have. This is easily done via e-mail or in a previous class session.
2. Select topics for the small groups based on the results of this survey.
3. Determine the questions to which the small groups will respond.
4. Identify key points to be emphasized in follow-up discussion.
5. Prepare handouts with database descriptions or other resources students will use.

Class Instructions

Provide class with a general introduction/orientation to the library, including Library of Congress classification and Subject Headings. Focus on how this facilitates access to materials of all kinds. The online catalog and electronic database network are also introduced with particular emphasis on what types of information can be found in each. In order to provide a context for the activity, discuss research as a circular process requiring definition of the topic/question, identification of relevant information, location of the information and evaluation of both the information itself and the process.

The class is randomly divided into 4–5 small groups by having them count off. Each group selects its own reporter and is assigned one of the topics based on the earlier student survey. The groups are asked to respond to the following questions with regard to their assigned topic:
- Is the topic manageable? If not, what would make it manageable?
- Which indexes/databases would you choose to use? Give your top three and defend your choices.
- What word(s) would you use to search each database?

Groups now have about 20 minutes to formulate responses to these questions. The course instructor and the session instructor circulate among the groups providing guidance and keeping the groups on task. After it is clear that all groups have worked through all the questions, the class reassembles and the reporter for each group presents the rest of the class with the answers they determined for their assigned topic.

Several important points emerged in the course of discussing each group's results with the class. First, manageability is difficult for students to determine. For purposes of this exercise, the instructor may need to clearly give students permission to narrow the topic in whatever way they like while in their small groups. Further questioning or refinements about the breadth of the topic, pointing out various aspects of the topic students may not have considered, may be necessary as part of the discussion. Students will often see during this refinement stage the need to gather additional information in order to understand the topic sufficiently to be able to narrow it. Suggestions for ways of finding this additional information other than in periodical indexes is often helpful.

Second, although students are primarily first-year students, choice of database is invariably toward the more specialized databases, such as *Medline, Biological Abstracts,* or *Wildlife & Fisheries Review.* It is necessary to highlight the usefulness of more easily accessible databases, such *as General Science Index, Applied Science & Technology Index,* or *Periodical Abstracts.* An important point to be brought out here is that the databases that are more accessible to undergraduates are also the ones for which the library owns a larger percentage of the material covered. This makes finding the full articles easier.

A further point is that based on the database descriptions, students do not always realize that nearly any index may have information on a given topic, but that each index has a built-in perspective that can help to focus their research. Popular topics often involve economic aspects of environmental issues, but students seldom choose to look in the *Business Periodicals Index* until this point is brought out.

In discussing the words to use in each database, students tend to want to include every word they determine relevant within each database. It is helpful to point out the necessity of using the perspective of the database to help refine and limit what words to use. Use of terms such as "environment" in an ecologically focused database or "economics" in a business database are less useful than "environment" in the business database or "economics" in the ecology database. It is also helpful to discuss the need to identify the primary concepts of the topic as well as synonyms for those concepts in order to gain the maximum amount of relevant information from the search.

I found that by the time a couple of groups had reported and their ideas had been discussed, the reporters for the later groups took it on themselves to modify what they had been going to report. They had clearly related what had been discussed and suggestions that had been made to their own topic.

Each of the ideas above needs to be related back to the goal of defining, identifying, locating, and evaluating each step as a circular process that can double back at any point. Students gained from the ideas that research is not linear, it requires critical evaluation all along the way, and that all databases are not equal.

52. Computer Science Library Resources Challenge

Holle E. Schneider
University of South Carolina-Spartanburg

Introduction

Few courses in computer science require students to visit the library. For the relatively rare computer science courses that do require a research paper, this exercise will expose students to a wide range of library resources that might help them with their research. Students enjoy the challenge of competing with others to try to find as many answers as possible. It is unlikely that students will ever find all of the answers in the time allotted.

Name tags for students with the team designation will foster a sense of cooperation in the team and signal reference staff that students are working on a class exercise. During the exercise, it is helpful to circulate to answer questions and provide hints, if needed.

Subject

Computer science

Level of Activity

Intermediate

Time Required

Preparation (first time only): 1–2 hours to adapt handouts provided in Figures 52-1 and 52-2; In-class: 30 minutes for activity, 20 minutes for discussion

Size of Class

Up to 30 (depending on size of reference area: 2–15 groups of 2–3 students each)

Preparation

1. (First time only) Adapt the Computer Science Library Resources Challenge sheet (Figure 52-1) and Computer Science Library Resources handout (Figure 52-2) as needed for your own library's collection.
2. Photocopy one Challenge sheet for each <u>team</u> (2-3 students).
3. Photocopy one Resources sheet for each <u>student</u> in the class.
4. Prepare team identification tags for each student. Teams can be identified by letters, colors, or computer companies (e.g., Apple, IBM, Compaq, Microsoft).

Class Instructions   You will have the next 30 minutes to work with your team to complete the Computer Science Library Resources Challenge. First, choose a team captain to assign and record answers to the 12 questions on the challenge sheet. Work as quickly as you can, but do not be concerned if you do not answer every question. At [set time (allow 30 minutes)], we will return to [set location] to discuss the resources you used to answer the questions.

Discussion   Divide students in groups of 2 or 3, by handing out tags randomly and allowing teams to find each other in the classroom. Hand out the resources sheets to all students. When team captains have been selected, give them the Challenge sheets. Ask them to assign questions to students in the group and discuss possible resources to check, then record answers when they are found. You will circulate among the teams to answer any questions about the resources and give hints as needed to keep the momentum of the exercise going.

After 30 minutes, gather the class and recap any questions that were asked during the exercise from which the whole class will benefit. Figure 52-3 provides partial answers to the challenge questions. Using the challenge questions as examples, explain the benefits of the major computer science resources and discuss how they might be used for more in-depth research. Handouts for the exercise to be adapted for the individual institution follow. It is preferable to keep the list brief and focused on the sources that will be most useful for the specific research assignment.

FIGURE 52-1
Sample Challenge Questions

COMPUTER SCIENCE LIBRARY RESOURCES CHALLENGE

Following are questions that are designed to expose you to some of the library's major resources for computer science: the book catalog, periodical indexes, reference books, and circulating books.

As team captain, you will assign the questions to your teammates, help them review the list of resources for possible places to start, and record their answers. Work as quickly as you can, but do not be concerned if you do not find all of the answers.

The librarian is available to answer any questions you have about the resources.

1. In the field of computing, what does FDC stand for? (Are there different answers?)

2. In which call number range(s) do you find the library's books on the Internet?

3. Does the library own any books on/about computers in the browsing collection? If yes, please give the citation to any one of them.

4. Approximately how many periodicals does the library own in the subject area of computer science?

5. If you are trying to find articles on the topic of artificial intelligence, will you find more citations in the *General Science Index* or in *ProQuest Periodical Abstracts Research*? (This might be considered a "trick question.")

FIGURE 52-1 cont.

6. Give the citation to a recent article on artificial intelligence that you can find in this library's holdings.

7. How many modes of searching the book catalog are there? Please list them.

8. What command would you use to search systemwide holdings in the book catalog (not just our library)?

9. How many books on the topic of <u>hackers</u> are retrieved in the book catalog? List a title if you find one.

10. List the call number ranges in which books on computers and computing are cataloged. (Hint: There is more than one.)

11. If you wanted to read an informative essay on cryptography and did not want to hunt for a journal article, where might you find such an article? (Please do not use a general encyclopedia.) If you find one, please list the citation.

12. I need a biography on John William Mauchly. Please find one for me and cite it here. (Please do not use a general encyclopedia.) (Hint: ENIAC was Mauchly's brainchild.)

FIGURE 52-2
Sample Computer Science Resource List

SELECTED COMPUTER SCIENCE LIBRARY RESOURCES

Dictionaries and Encyclopedias

Encyclopedia of Computer Science. Ed. Anthony Ralston, Edwin D. Reilly. 3d ed. New York: Van Nostrand Reinhold, 1993.

IBM Dictionary of Computing. Ed. George McDaniel. 10th ed., rev. New York: McGraw–Hill, 1993.

Prentice Hall's Illustrated Dictionary of Computing. New York: Prentice Hall, 1992.

Other Reference Sources

Computer Industry Almanac. Annual. Dallas, Tex.: Computer Industry Almanac.

Datapro Management of Microcomputer Systems. Monthly. Delran, N.J.: Datapro Research Corp.

Magill's Survey of Science. Applied Science Series. Ed. Frank N. Magill. Pasadena, Calif.: Salem Press, 1993.

Periodical Indexes

ACM Guide to Computing Literature. Monthly. New York: Association for Computing Machinery.

Applied Science & Technology Index. Monthly. New York: H. W. Wilson Co.

Computer & Control Abstracts. Monthly. London: Institution of Electrical Engineers.

Computer Literature Index. Monthly. Phoenix, Ariz.: Applied Computer Research.

General Science Index. Monthly. New York: H. W. Wilson Co.

Microcomputer Index. Monthly. Santa Clara, Calif.: Microcomputer Information Services.

Periodical Abstracts Ondisc. Monthly. Ann Arbor, Mich.: University Microfilms International.

Book Catalog

[Description and instructions for local online catalog]

Sample Library of Congress Subject Headings:

> *Expert systems (Computer science)*
> BT   *Artificial intelligence*
>   *Electronic data processing*
>   *Information storage and retrieval*
> NT   *ETS (Computer program)*
>   *Knowledge acquisition (Expert systems)*
>   *SOLOMON (Computer program)*
>   *View Creation System (Computer system)*
> —*Library applications*
> —*Validation*
> —*Verification*

FIGURE 52-3
Partial Answers to the Computer Science Library Resources Challenge

1. In the field of computing, what does FDC stand for? (Are there different answers?)

    Floppy disk controller (*Prentice Hall's Illustrated Dictionary of Computing*, p. 166)
    Frame dependent control mode (*IBM Dictionary of Computing*, p. 264)

2. In which call number range(s) do you find the library's books on the Internet?

    TK5105.5-TK5105.875
    HD30.335 (business)
    Z (library applications)

3. Does the library own any books on/about computers in the browsing collection? If
    yes, please give the citation to any one of them.

    [Site-specific, e.g., Carroll, Paul. *Big Blues: The Unmaking of IBM.* New York: Crown
    Publishers, 1993.]

4. Approximately how many periodicals does the library own in the subject area of
    computer science?

    [Site-specific, e.g., keyword in subject search for **computer? periodicals**, **minicom-
    puter? periodicals**, and **microcomputer? periodicals**]

5. If you are trying to find articles on the topic of artificial intelligence, will you find
    more citations in the *General Science Index* or in *ProQuest Periodical Abstracts Re-
    search*? (This might be considered a "trick question.")

    [Site-specific answer depending on databases and coverage. This could be consid-
    ered a "trick question" because students must take into account the time coverage
    of the database.]

6. Give the citation to a recent article on artificial intelligence that you can find in this
    library's holdings.

    [Site-specific, e.g., Langreth, Robert. "The Bad Boy of Robotics." *Popular Science*
    246 (June 1995): 44.]

FIGURE 52-3 cont.

7. How many modes of searching the book catalog are there? Please list them.

    [Site-specific, e.g., keyword, title, author, subject heading, call number]

8. What command would you use to search systemwide holdings in the book catalog (not just our library)?

    [Site-specific answer]

9. How many books on the topic of <u>hackers</u> are retrieved in the book catalog? List a title if you find one.

    [Site-specific, e.g., Hafner, Katie. *Cyberpunk: Outlaws and Hackers on the Computer Frontier.* New York: Simon & Schuster, 1991.]

10. List the call number ranges in which books on computers and computing are cataloged. (Hint: There is more than one.)

    QA76 – QA76.3 (mathematics)
    TK7885 – TK7895 (electrical engineering)

    Found in *Library of Congress Subject Headings* under "Computers."

11. If you wanted to read an informative essay on cryptography and did not want to hunt for a journal article, where might you find such an article? (Please do not use a general encyclopedia.) If you find one, please list the citation.

    Magill's Survey of Science. Applied Science Series, p. 579

12. I need a biography on John William Mauchly. Please find one for me and cite it here. (Please do not use a general encyclopedia.) (Hint: ENIAC was Mauchly's brain-child.)

    Encyclopedia of Computer Science, p. 833

---

53. Desparately Seeking Communication Information

Gail Gradowski
Santa Clara University, Santa Clara, California

Introduction   These exercises were designed for an upper-division communication theory class that is required to do a literature review. Depending on the specific topic being researched, students could be using a wide range of different information tools in a variety of disciplines. Three of the exercises had to do with this variety. The other two cover keyword searches and the intricacies of searching for periodicals in the online catalog.

Subject   Communication (Could be modified for other disciplines)

Level of Activity   Intermediate (Requires some experience using the online catalog and *Expanded Academic Index*)

Time Required   Preparation, 1–3 hours (first time only), in-class, 90+ minutes

Size of Class   25–30 students (In groups of 3, maximum depends on number of computers available)

Preparation   Meet with the faculty member to discuss the session and adapt it to the class. Adapt Figures 53-1 through 53-5 for your institution. The exercise sheets, especially Figure 53-5, "Do We Own It?", should include examples of sources that are difficult to find in your online catalog.

Arrange for the exercise sheets to be given out at the class meeting before the library session. It is absolutely critical that the exercise sheets be distributed ahead of time to the class and that the students be required to work on them individually before coming to the library. If they are done in the library session without much thought in the groups, there will be little for them to discuss in the groups, defeating much of the purpose and lowering the level of the discussion.

Set up the classroom to accommodate the number of groups required. Each group area should have a clean set of exercise sheets ready.

Class Instructions

Preliminaries It is best to group students as randomly as possible. This can be done by numbering tables/seats and giving students numbers as they enter the classroom.

Introduction Once students are in groups, the sessions begins with an introduction to literature reviews and the interdisciplinary nature of communication research. Presumably, their instructor has already talked to them about the whys and wherefores of doing a literature review, but it is good to ask them a few crucial questions, like, "Why bother doing a literature review?" Points relating the various exercises to the lit review can be made all at once at the start of the session or as the exercises are reviewed later.

Exercises Students are then instructed to take out their individual exercise sheets, completed before the class. Then, with each sheet, in the following order, students compare their individual answers in their groups and come up with a group answer and write it on the clean exercise sheet. Following are a suggested timetable for each exercise and some follow-up questions to be used with the class as a whole after each group works on the exercise.

Who do you want to hear from? (Figure 53-1) Allow 5–10 minutes for groups to reach consensus, 5 minutes to make a point about the interdisciplinary nature of communication research, and randomly select a few students to tell the class their topic and have the class relate that to academic disciplines.

Match game (Figure 53-2) Allow 5–10 minutes for groups to reach consensus, 10 minutes to select a few items on the list to make points about the value of bibliographies, annual reviews, and encyclopedias; locating these items; and the types of periodicals and their uses.

Match game II (Figure 53-3) Allow 5–10 minutes for groups to reach consensus, 5–10 minutes for discussion of any Column A to Column B problem items (there are usually a few that they cannot agree on) and to make sure everyone has figured out where each index is indeed located.

Keyword searches (Figure 53-4) Allow 10 minutes for groups to get a good start on these. As they are working, select various groups and answers to use in the follow-up discussion. Usually there are some great examples out there. Have people from various groups write their best answer on the board for the ones that you have selected. The goals here are to demonstrate several crucial points, such as deciding on the best words to use in keyword searches, the need to do multiple searches, and constructing a complex search statement by nesting terms in and/or combinations.

Do we own it? (Figure 53–5) Time allowed for this one depends on what is left. If there is sufficient time, groups could review the answers where they do not have consensus at an OPAC terminal. This would take about 10 minutes. Follow-up discussion would then be about the ones they did not find. The main point to make here is that students often give up too fast when trying to determine what the library owns.

Discussion

This series of exercises can be difficult to orchestrate. Careful time-keeping is important to keep the class moving along. If more or less time is available, things can be cut, additional points can be added, or additional activities can be incorporated, such as group hands-on work with specific tools, especially various indexes.

The one most important thing to try to fit in is *Communication Abstracts*, especially because students find using a paper index particularly frustrating.

FIGURE 53-1

WHO DO YOU WANT TO HEAR FROM?

When doing communication research, you soon discover that it is often multidisciplinary. The topics you are researching often are multifaceted, of interest to many different people. To do a thorough job of it then, you must first consider exactly WHO you want to hear from. That will then determine where you will need to look.

So, for each of the possible communication research topics described below, list all of the academic disciplines that would have something to contribute to its study.

use of environmental claims in product advertising

value of employee suggestion boxes

gorilla–human communication

Ronald Reagan as the great communicator

persuasion in therapeutic communication

FIGURE 53-2

THE MATCH GAME

This exercise is a test of your expectations. You must think about where you might expect to find some information. Match the information need in column A with the publication title in column B that you might expect to find the information in.

Column A

review of the literature/research on language and "world view" (jargon for culture)

review of the literature/research on gender, power, and communication in organizations

short history of photojournalism (highlights, landmarks, etc.)

report of a research study of 6-9 year old children, specific TV programs/characters and risk-taking behavior

an editorial critical of Rush Limbaugh

an editorial praising Rush Limbaugh

speech by Shelly Schwab (president of MCATV, Universal Studios) at NYU on television in the '90s (sometime in the spring, I think)

scholarly article analyzing media rhetoric on harmful rap music lyrics

list of all the significant writings on marketing to children published between 1960 and 1990

the name of THE authority on subliminal messages

recent statistics, state-by-state, on new business starts and business failures, by year

Column B

Bibliography of Research and Writings on Marketing and Advertising to Children (a reference book)

Mother Jones (a periodical)

Progress in Communication Science (an annual review)

Encyclopedia of Psychology (reference book)

American Social Behavior (a periodical)

Vital Speeches of the Day (a periodical)

Statistical Abstract of the United States (an annual reference book)

Annual Review of Anthropology (an annual review)

Journal of Experimental Child Psychology (a periodical)

International Encyclopedia of Communications (reference book)

American Spectator (a periodical)

FIGURE 53–3

THE MATCH GAME II

This exercise tests your ability to guess where the information you need might be hiding. After all, unless you can do that, you'll never find it, will you? Match the information need in column A with the index/catalog in column B that you would use to look for it.

BONUS POINTS:
• For each of the indexes listed in Column B, indicate whether it is available in computerized form, or not (Y/N).
• For each of the indexes that is available in computerized form, indicate which service you would use to access it: I (InfoTrac), C (CD-ROM network), F (FirstSearch).

Column A	Column B
recent review article on communication patterns of AIDS patients and their caregivers/family/friends	*Sociological Abstracts*
reviews of a recent controversial book on violence in television	*Monthly Catalog of U.S. Government Documents*
reports of recent research on gender differences in persuasive speech	Online catalog
results of a Department of Education survey on adult literacy	*Index Medicus*
recent academic journal article on television political advertisements from the point of view of a political science professor	*ABI/Inform*
update a 1991 bibliography on marketing to children	*PAIS Expanded Academic Index*
	Communication Abstracts
	PsycLIT

FIGURE 53-4

KEYWORD SEARCHES

How good are YOU at talking to the computer?

Whether you are using the online catalog or InfoTrac or FirstSearch, to do a thorough and effective job of it, you absolutely, positively MUST do KEYWORD searches.

For each of the possible communication research topics below, write the best possible keyword search you can come up with. You might want to also consider whether you would need to do more than one. If so, feel free to write more than one. You might also want to try them out in Expanded Academic Index, for example.

images of Native Americans on TV

gorilla-human communication

Ronald Reagan as the great communicator

Cosby show and the image of African-American families on TV

military "control" of the news during the Persian Gulf War

FIGURE 53-5

DO WE OWN IT?

These citations are taken from a variety of computer and non-computer indexes. Check the online catalog to determine which ones you could expect to find in the library.

Cited in *Communication Abstracts*: 133 Stiff, J. B., Kim, H. J., and Ramesh, C. N. Truth biases and aroused suspicion in relational deception. Communication Research 19(3):326–345, June 1992

Do we own it?   Yes   No

If so, where is it located?
   Periodicals, by title   Periodicals, by call number   Other (describe)

Cited in *Expanded Academic Index:* Assessing the constitutionality of press restrictions in the Persian Gulf War. Matthew J. Jacobs. *Stanford Law Review*, Fall 1992 v44 n1 p675(52).

Do we own it?   Yes   No

If so, where is it located?
   Periodicals, by title   Periodicals, by call number   Other (describe)

Cited in *PAIS Decade* on FirstSearch:
PAIS NO: 91-1211489
AUTHOR: Williams, Pete
TITLE: The press and the Persian Gulf war
JOURNAL: (*Parameters*) 21:2-9 Autumn 1991
YEAR: 1991
PUBL TYPE: Periodical article
LANGUAGE: English

Do we own it?   Yes   No

If so, where is it located?
   Periodicals, by title   Periodicals, by call number   Other (describe)

FIGURE 53-5 cont.

Cited in *Sociological Abstracts* on FirstSearch:
NUMBER: 89U4061
AUTHOR(S): Bogart, Leo
TITLE: The Multiple Meanings of Television Advertising
PUB YEAR: 1988
JOURNAL: *Society*, 1988, 25, 4(174), May-June, 76–80.
STANDARD NO:CODEN: SOCYA6

Do we own it?   Yes   No

If so, where is it located?
    Periodicals, by title   Periodicals, by call number   Other (describe)

Cited in *PsycLIT*:
TI: Source effects in communication and persuasion research: A meta-analysis of effect size.
AU: Wilson,-Elizabeth-J.; Sherrell,-Daniel-L. IN: Louisiana State U, US JN: *Journal-of-the-Academy-of-Marketing-Science*; 1993 Spr Vol 21(2) 101–112

Do we own it?   Yes   No

If so, where is it located?
    Periodicals, by title   Periodicals, by call number   Other (describe)

Cited in *Communication Abstracts* 1233: Pecora, N. Superman/superboys/supermen: the comic book hero as socializing agent. Craig, S., ed. *Men, Masculinity, and the Media.* Newbury Park, CA: Sage Publications, 1992, pp. 61–77. $42.00

Do we own it?   Yes   No

If so, where is it located?
    Periodicals, by title   Periodicals, by call number   Other (describe)

Cited in *Communication Abstracts* 207: Liska, J. Dominance-seeking language strategies: please eat the floor, dogbreath, or I'll rip your lungs out, okay? Deetz, S.A., ed. *Communication Yearbook* 15. Newbury Park, CA: Sage Publications, 1992, pp. 427–456. $65.00

Do we own it?   Yes   No

If so, where is it located?
    Periodicals, by title   Periodicals, by call number   Other (describe)

54. Introducing Women's Studies Resources

Lucretia McCulley
Boatwright Library, University of Richmond, Richmond, Virginia

---

Introduction

This exercise has three parts, which can be used separately or as a series in three classes. The goals of each part follow:

A. To introduce the many journal titles available in women's studies

B. To introduce specialized indexes and to demonstrate that many women's studies topics are not covered in commonly available indexes and databases

C. To introduce the wide variety of women's studies reference sources

Subject

Women's studies

Level of Activity

Intermediate

Time Required

Preparation, 2–3 hours; in-class, 20–30 minutes for each of the three parts

Size of Class

15–20 students

Preparation

A. Journals

Gather enough issues of women's studies journals for each group to have one to examine.

Class Instructions

1. Divide the class into groups of 2–3 and give each group a journal to examine.

2. Ask students to consider the following questions:
- What is the purpose of the journal?
- In what year did it begin publication?
- Is it scholarly, trade, or popular?
- Could this journal be of use to you in your personal or academic life?

3. Ask each group to report to the class on its findings.

B. Women's Studies Abstracts

Preparation

1. Select topics that show a notable difference in coverage in *Women's Studies Abstracts* and a general index like *Readers' Guide*.

2. Prepare photocopy samples or an overhead transparency to explain how to read index citations from each index.

3. Gather enough volumes of each index for each group to have a volume of each to examine.

Class Instructions

1. Divide the class into groups of 2–3 and give each group index volumes to examine.

2. Introduce a sample topic. Explain how to find citations in each index on that topic and read the citations.

3. Ask students to search the indexes and compare the number of citations for the topic.

4. Show students where the list of journals indexed can be found in each index and ask them to compare the journal coverage. Is there an overlap between the two indexes?

5. Ask each group to report to the class on its findings.

C. Reference Sources

Preparation

Gather a selection of reference books, such as statistical works, chronologies, handbooks, biographical directories, and encyclopedias in the area of women's studies.

Class Instructions

1. Divide the class into groups of 2–3 and give each group a reference book to examine.

2. Ask students to consider the following questions:
• What is the purpose of the book?
• What kind of information does it provide?
• Is it user-friendly?
• What special contribution does this source provide for women's studies?

3. Ask each group to report to the class on its findings.